Equal Partnering:
A Feminine Perspective

Equal Partnering: A Feminine Perspective

Barbara Jo Brothers
Editor

Equal Partnering: A Feminine Perspective, edited by Barbara Jo Brothers, was simultaneously issued by The Haworth Press, Inc., under the same title, as a special issue of the *Journal of Couples Therapy*, Volume 2, Number 4 1991.

Harrington Park Press
An Imprint of
The Haworth Press, Inc.
New York • London

AAZ 4999

ISBN 1 56023-017-7

Published by

Harrington Park Press, 10 Alice Street, Binghamton, NY 13904-1580

Harrington Park Press is an imprint of The Haworth Press, Inc., 10 Alice Street, Binghamton, NY 13904-1580 USA

Equal Partnering: A Feminine Perspective has also been published as *Journal of Couples Therapy*, Volume 2, Number 4 1991.

Library of Congress Cataloging-in-Publication Data

Equal partnering : a feminine perspective / Barbara Jo Brothers, editor.
    p. cm.
    "Also . . . published as Journal of couples therapy, volume 2, number 4, 1991" – T.p. verso.
    Includes bibliographical references.
    ISBN 1-56024-260-4 (alk. paper). – ISBN 1-56023-017-7 (pbk. : alk. paper)
    1. Marital psychotherapy. 2. Man-woman relationships. I. Brothers, Barbara, 1940- .
RC488.5.E68 1992
616.89'156 – dc20

                                      92-13454
                                         CIP

Equal Partnering:
A Feminine Perspective

CONTENTS

ABOUT THE EDITOR

Barbara Jo Brothers, MSW, BCD, a Diplomate in Clinical Social Work, National Association of Social Workers, is in private practice in New Orleans. She received her BA from the University of Texas and her MSW from Tulane University, where she is currently on the faculty. She was editor of *The Newsletter of the American Academy of Psychotherapists* from 1976 to 1985, and was associate editor of *Voices: The Art and Science of Psychotherapy* from 1979 to 1989. She has nearly 30 years of experience, in both the public and private sectors, helping people to form skills that will enable them to connect emotionally. The author of numerous articles and book chapters on authenticity in human relating, she has advocated healthy, congruent communication that builds intimacy as opposed to destructive, incongruent communication which blocks intimacy. In addition to her many years of direct work with couples and families, Ms. Brothers has led numerous workshops on teaching communication in families and has also played an integral role in the development of training programs in family therapy for mental health workers throughout the Louisiana state mental health system. She is a board member of the Institute for International Connections, a non-profit organization for cross-cultural professional development, focused on training and cross-cultural exchange with psychotherapists in Russia, republics once part of what used to be the Soviet Union, and other Eastern European countries.

Equal Partnering:
A Feminine Perspective

The Constructive Use of Power
and the Philosophy of the Self
in the Training of Family Therapists

Barbara Jo Brothers

. . . These kinds of control/power problems [among family therapists] are based upon fear, fear 'I won't be valued or loved' . . .

Virginia Satir 1985

(Ed. note: The following is a reflection on "Power Issues in Therapists," the transcript of the interview with Virginia Satir which appears in this volume.)

Virginia understood therapy to be a meeting of the deepest *self* of the therapist with the deepest *self* of the patient (Satir, 1987, p. 24). For such a meeting to take place, there are certain prerequisites having to do with how these two selves feel about themselves; the level of self-esteem not only in the patient, but also in the therapist. The human experience being what it is and psychotherapists being, in fact, members of the human race, self-esteem issues in the therapist can be barriers to that deep meeting of selves.

The following are examples. If I, as therapist, allow my *self-esteem* to hinge on the work I am doing with a couple or to hinge on whether or not they "love" me during a given session, the therapy may be adversely affected in a number of ways: (1) I can be so occupied with my own anxiety I do not receive the information that would allow me to "see" the deep selves of the couple before me; (2) I can falsely reassure myself by facilitating their "one-downness" and looking exclusively at their pathology; they may, in response, oblige me by *showing* me only the pathology and not the

1

deep selves; (3) I can stay entirely in my head so as to avoid *any* troublesome feelings and nothing but intellect is visible on either side; (4) I can leave the subject completely and suggest that, instead, we do tarot card readings or something; again, deep selves — not being taken seriously — would stay tucked away.

Or, I can plumb my own depths, locate and own my doubts and look back to the messages I got in my family of origin to account for whatever specific wilting I begin to feel as the couple engage in certain interactions. With a commitment to self exploration, I do not have to visit my own power and control issues on my patients; I will not be so easily tempted to make myself feel powerful at their expense or feel threatened by a momentary sense of my own powerlessness occurring in a particular session.

Like a symphony of fine instruments, we have, in Virginia's mind, only to be tuned — first to ourselves, then with one another.

Virginia's focus, in all her training, on the self of the therapist was due to her awareness of the link between internal feelings of self-worth, rules of the particular family system within which a given person was reared, and external modes of communication. Conscious use of self was the underpinning of her therapy as well as her training of therapists; awareness that one's own feelings of self-worth at a given moment are a pivotal factor in the effective, constructive use of self. The awareness of one's feelings *about* one's feelings is the source of authentic personal power.

I cannot enter the consulting room with only the left half of my brain and hang my feelings on a hook somewhere outside the door. Even though such vivisection is no longer seriously advocated as in the psychoanalytic days of yore, there remains considerable bias in our culture toward a linear, cause-and-effect model of thinking — and a great nescience that holding this model constitutes being "scientific" and/or psychologically "mature." This attitude permits the premise that the *cognitive* information about behavior constitutes the only "real" therapeutic situation.

Virginia emphasized the importance of recognizing *three* kinds of information.

> In information, there is (1) cognitive information, there is (2) emotional information, and there is (3) sensual information. (Satir, 1987, tape 5)

This is another example of the importance of wholeness, the importance of not leaving out any of the integral pieces, and the importance of the body as a part of the information matrix — the use of the *whole* self instead of the intellect only.

> *In the Western world we have given most of our attention to cognitive information.* We read it in a book, we see the words, and the words make the images, but reading it in a book doesn't show how the person is feeling or thinking or how they are gesturing or how they are breathing . . . so it is a totally different thing when we put it into a human context.
>
> I want to give you just enough so that we get a good context for this. If you will remember, when I use information, it is on *all* levels . . . It is not about just giving words. (Satir, 1987, tape 5)

Most of our culture, which is not particularly psychologically oriented, is not tuned in to that *emotional* information about which Virginia is talking. And that can make the vital difference. Blocking awareness of emotional information blocks awareness of our nature as whole beings. Refusing to allow into consciousness the emotional information, which includes the way my emotions are responding in the therapy context, makes an obstacle to awareness of the points at which my own issues — left over from my primary triad in my family of origin — are being triggered.

The linear model of mechanistic thinking, focused only on the cognitive and in which one looks for "the problem" and "the solution," gives an illusion of safety through order. Indeed, we have read in the papers that some in what used to be the Soviet Union still state a wish to go back to the old days of "law and order" when life was predictable and the same number of rubles bought the same number of potatoes. Of course, one need look no farther for an example of where such a concentration on *task* — on order in the context — costs dearly for the individual human beings involved. Allowing awareness of the worth of the individual to slip, in the collective mind, to lower priority than "the task" provides a clear road for some rather profound consequences. Wholeness, the valuing of *all* aspects of the human being — cognitive, emotional, and sensual — is not a luxury in our modern world where almost no population is farther away than a computer keyboard and the triggers on everybody's bombs get hairier every year . . .

One does not, however, have to be an axe murderer, international terrorist, notorious dictator or a cocky prima donna family therapist to retain a destructive philosophy of self. One may simply be reared with a "good" religious background: Buddhist or Baptist, one can hear among most such folk the fear and loathing of "ego" and "selfishness," as if dispensing with all thought of self would turn the pious toward holiness and away from evil. From the latest popes to the latest maharishis, most of humanity has been taught to confuse authentic self-regard with the attitude of the disdaining narcissist. Consequently, both that one who aspires to altruism as well as the disdaining narcissist are given few guidelines, as each passes through society's various institutions, about the healing nature of *connecting* with other human beings as opposed to the manipulation of them.

Knowing the development of self-worth to be an uphill battle against centuries of teaching of misinformation, Virginia understood:

> There is no question in my mind . . . that everybody has self-worth. But very few people know it. And so letting that self-worth come out is going to make that person whole. *No highly developed self-worth is ever destructive.* When we were kids we were told not to be selfish. Well, you see that would mean we would be selfish *when we didn't have our worth*, and we had to develop all those manipulations in order to live. That's what [incongruent] communication is about. (Banmen and Satir, 1983, p. 85)

Virginia knew that training the family therapist (or, in her words, the "change agent") in awareness of that person's *own* uniqueness would both enrich the therapist and protect the patient from being disempowered. That which builds self-worth is inherently empowering.

> There's another word I love very much which is . . . *empowerment.* Empowerment is what we do to eliminate enslavement.

We can enslave ourselves with our thoughts: "I'm no good. Who wants to have anything to do with me?" We can empower ourselves by saying: "I'm just a fine person and I'm ready to say what isn't so hot about me and so on. It's okay." . . . I am working toward the empowerment of every human being that I can possibly touch and that includes me. Empowerment comes when we have been able to heal, in our mind, the primary triad [of the family of origin] . . . Until we do that healing, life will always be a divided thing for us. (Satir, 1987, tape 2)

That was the way Virginia connected power and the philosophy of self.

Neither was Virginia's awareness of self-worth a simple-minded "let's be always positive" and it did *not* mean closing one's ears and eyes to information about one's own behavior that had potential to be self- (and other-) destructive. She believed that growth and self-worth were a matched team; one does not go without the other.

The idea was to learn to receive criticism, for example, as information — "as a light bulb, rather than a black mark" (Virginia Satir, personal communication, August, 1971).

One of the questions we have to ask ourselves at the time when we want to decide whether [what we are experiencing] is the pain of blame or the pain of recognition is: "Am I a good person?" [and to answer] "I think I am a good person." . . . Close your eyes and let yourself know that there is *a latitude for you to remain with the feeling of goodness inside yourself as a result of your pure spirit while open to the possibilities that you sometimes learn [about] things that aren't so good for you* . . . when you find out about [those things] you can let [them] go . . . (emphasis added) (Satir, 1987, tape 2)

Virginia considered awareness of "what is" to be essential to the training process, to the therapy process, and to all other human processes.

Of course, Virginia was very interested in facilitating the processing of information — and knew it was often blocked by the attempt of the person to protect the often emotionally and psychologically battered self. Ever mindful of wanting to provide experiences in wholeness, Virginia would help people tune in to their physical responses in a given interaction to provide another route for accessing information:

> Think of your body as a constant and continual live, responding and sending station, moving all the time. This body is this wonderful sending and receiving instrument. (Satir, 1987, tape 2)

Knowing that the protection of the delicate self inside is of crucial importance, Virginia would guide the therapist-in-training toward greater awareness of the interior processes of both self and other — providing access to the information while providing a means for self protection at the same time.

For example, on projection:

> . . . we can be anxious inside. Now, that rolls around in all kinds of different ways. However, the feeling of being *sent* something from someone [differs from] the anxiety that you get when you send things to yourself (you know, "I'm not doing it right" and "Who is going to love me?" and all that kind of stuff). That piece [the self-worth dialogue in parenthesis] is your *own* anxiety. We need to learn to separate what is coming from the inside from what is coming from the outside. I can tell the difference in my body between whether or not I am reacting to my own anxiety or responding to something coming from the outside.
>
> That gets finely tuned; but actually, when you learn how to *center* and you can feel your own breathing, then it is like something is acting upon you and you know that it is something [coming] from the *other* person . . .
>
> . . . It isn't as hard as it sounds, but when people use so much cognitive stuff without knowing about what else is going on, they make so many mistakes. (Satir, 1987, tape 2)

This news about tuning in to the body for clues would be particularly important for the therapist more naturally given to (or conditioned to) relying on the intellect — which accounts for a large percentage of the world's psychotherapists.

The above quotation, taken from a transcription of one of Virginia's training seminars through an Avanta Process Community is an example of her emphasis on the importance of teaching about the philosophy of the self. It is also an example of her understanding that addressing *wholeness* means to expand learning beyond simply the imparting of *cognitive* information.

Virginia's system of training was such that "you had to be there" to experience learning on all the levels necessary for doing respectful work with people.[1] Just as therapy cannot take place simply by reading a book on one's particular issues, learning about the deep level of connecting which is possible between human beings is not obtainable solely through books or even videotapes. Her training included the student's work, through the family reconstruction vehicle, on his/her own primary triad.

Virginia envisioned a world in which therapists would have come to understand the old, dysfunctional messages received in their family of origin/primary triad, to understand the inhuman rules which the great majority of us were reared to apply to ourselves, and to be, therefore, in a position to free our patients from the tyranny. Such therapists would serve as models, working cooperatively and in partnership rather than being caught up in the spiraling treadmill of competitive behavior. Life might be experienced in a much more celebratory fashion if it were not perceived as a desperate race to get ahead of the other.

Couples experiencing the therapists who value cooperation more than competition could have, therefore, a model for life as equals rather than a preoccupation with who runs the show. All the destructive "isms" would atrophy if the competitive "who's got the power" focus could be widely replaced with a model of *mutual* empowerment which follows mutual respect for the uniqueness of each separate self in any dyad.

It was Virginia's belief and experience that this respect naturally follows those encounters between deepest self of the one with deepest self of the other. She based her own training of psychotherapists on that belief.

NOTE

1. For this reason, the therapist who wants to have an in-depth understanding of the Satir model would do well to attend one of the longer seminars provided by members of the Avanta Network.

REFERENCES

Satir, V. (1967) A family of angels. pg. 97-173. In *techniques of family therapy* eds. Haley, J. and Hoffman, L. New York: Harper Torchbooks.

Banmen, J. and Satir, V. (1983) *Virginia Satir verbatim*. John Banmen. Delta Psychological Associates, Inc. 11213 Canyon Crescent, North Delta, British Columbia, Canada V4E 2R6.

Satir, V. (1985). Speaker. An Interview with Virginia Satir by Sheldon Starr, PhD. (Available from Sheldon Starr, PhD., 801 Welch Road, #209, Palo Alto, California 94304).

Satir, V. (1987). Speaker. Avanta Process Community VII, Module I. Cassette Recordings Nos. 2 & 5. Crested Butte, Colorado: Blue Moon Cassettes.

Satir, V. (1987). The therapist story. *The Journal of Psychotherapy and the Family, 3* (1), 17-25.

Satir, V. (1988). *The New Peoplemaking*. Mountain View, Ca: Science and Behavior Books.

Poem

That I am here
In this tight house
With this good man
with these nice kids
with these old friends
this fine food
these warm clothes
and not
                  in an earthquake
or a revolution
                  or a prison
or a plague

puzzles me.

                  —Judith Morley

Judith Morley, 250 Scudders Lane, Roslyn Harbor, NY 11576. Copyright 1992 Judith Morley.

Partnership and Ego Equality
in the Marital System

Barbara J. Lynch

SUMMARY. Ego equality, a term originating with the author, is the individual's ability to be a peer and to engage in peer interactions. This ability is a basic factor of dyadic systems. However, it is a factor that is often overlooked because of its apparent simplicity. Ego equality is presented here to accent the importance of the concept and to reinforce the significance of cross-gender partnership as a core issue in all work with couples.

The dyadic system is examined in terms of hierarchical structure. In addition the historical antecedents of inequitable structures are explored in the context of families of origin and other social systems. Disturbances in peer interactions are viewed as the foundation of symptom such as excessive non-productive conflict, unsatisfying sexual relations, and a loss of intimacy. Other therapeutic considerations are included.

INTRODUCTION

The marital system is multi-tiered and each stratum is interacting with and impacting on every other. The complexity of this system is appreciated when the interactive process of this stratification is understood. While factors are isolated here for purposes of clarity, the concepts of mutual interaction and reciprocity must be constantly reinforced.

Marital systems appear to thrive in an atmosphere of partnership characterized by basic ego equality between the partners. The individuals' ability to interact as peers, emotional equals, determines the overall style, tone, and direction of the relationship. This single

Barbara J. Lynch, PhD, is affiliated with Southern Connecticut State University, 501 Crescent Street, New Haven, CT 06515.

factor permeates all other elements of the couple's relationship and operates as a guiding principle for all transactions. Intimacy, power, sexual relations, and conflict are each affected by the degree to which the partnership is constructed according to the principles of equality.

The essence of a functional partnership is based on respect, on the concept that the partner has an intrinsic value. In the healthy relationship there is tangible evidence that each holds the other in high esteem and this regard is clearly distinct from unrealistic worship built on projections. The partners have earned each other's appreciation based on concrete data. When this partnership of equality exists, the individuals view each other as peers. In the intimate relationship between peers, there is apt to be an absence of the insecurity and anxiety commonly associated with being involved with someone who is seen as superior. Similarly, there is also an avoidance of the anger and resentment commonly found when in association with an inferior. The functional regulation of anxiety and anger paves the way for the building of intimacy vital to the marriage.

BACKGROUND

A relationship between peers does not spring into existence spontaneously. In fact, there may be some precedence for assuming that neither males nor females are inherently able to interact across gender lines as equals. In describing this phenomena from the viewpoint of Transactional Analysis and Berne's ego states, (Berne, 1961), the concept of non-equal interactions is more readily seen. From this theory the individual has three primary modes of response sets: responses from the 'Parent' ego state, the 'Adult' ego state and the 'Child' ego state. Parallel transactions are those which take place from one ego state in an individual to the same ego state in the partner. These would be peer transactions: interactions from Parent to Parent, Adult to Adult, Child to Child. Hoerwitz, (1981) states that all "positive," growth-oriented, and fun outcomes have their roots in parallel transactions" (1981, p. 60). Complimentary transactions are those which are sent from one ego state intended for another in a lesser or greater condition of power and control. These skewed power transactions would include Parent to Child, or Child to Parent. They always involve a statement about power and control along with a content message. For example a transaction from Child to Parent might be "Mama, may I go outside to play?" where the child is clearly in a one-down position, needing permission from the powerful parent to engage in an activity. The parent has control and may or may not grant the child's request. The appropriateness of the response is not dependent on the ego state, but rather on the context. However, if the parent replies from a Child ego state, it is an inappropriate transaction. The response might be, "Let's you and me play instead. Want to get a game?" In such a case there is no clear hierarchy and the transaction will be incomplete, inappropriate and can easily disintegrate into a struggle.

Taken alone, or occuring only on occasion, these transactions create no major difficulty. However, when they represent a rigid way of being, a non-flexible attitudinal posture which prevails in almost all situations, no matter what the context, then it is apt to create primary and pervasive disturbances in all areas of sub-system functioning. When a transactional style becomes a posture, it is usually the result of a learned response set which then forms the template for all interactions. Most of this is learned in the confines of the family system from significant models: mother's and father's interaction with each other; mother's and father's interactions with sons and daughters, (and the differences among these); and from the interaction between siblings.

In examining the possibilities from this model, a pattern becomes clear which forms the basis for the hypothesis that males and females may have an inherent difficulty in relating as peers. The most comfortable, i.e., natural stance for females to adopt in relationships with males may be that of superior, even though this superiority may be disguised. Females who protect men, those who allow men to be dominant, and those who nurture men, do so from a position of superiority. The protection and nurturance can be covertly or overtly masqueraded as consideration, thoughtfulness, or a sensitivity to masculine feelings. However, beneath the surface, there is conveyed an innate sense of the inferior status of men and an attentiveness to the fragile nature of the emotions and psyche of the male when transactions represent a stance which would not be naturally adopted in dealing with a female peer. Some of the beliefs held by females which support their view of men as inferiors or subordinates are:

1. Males are expected to be less skilled in domestic areas.
2. Men need more consideration and attention than women.
3. Women can easily hurt a man's feelings, and so, around men, women must monitor their own expressiveness.
4. Men are more emotionally fragile than women.
5. Men really never grow up.
6. It is easier to let men have their own way. They are not worthy opponents.
7. Men are bullies.
8. Women help men get where they are even if they don't get any of the credit.
9. There is always a hidden obligation or expectation when a man helps a woman.
10. Men cannot deal with competing with a woman, therefore women should never engage in competition with men.

When these beliefs operate in tandem with specific family of origin patterns, the result may be a rigid style of female one-up-manship. Girls who were groomed to care for their brothers were indoctrinated into non-peer interactions in the natural peer group. Whether the brothers were older or younger, if the girl was expected to do chores from which her brothers were exempted by virtue of their gender, the female began to experience herself as a nurturer and a caretaker. Both of these roles describe transactions between Parent and Child, a definite condition of hierarchy with executives and subordinates. In interactions of this nature, occuring in the sibling subsystem, a peer unit, it does not matter if the sister is in the ego-position of benevolent or critical Parent. What shapes the future of relationships is that male and female children are not naturally in the- same hierarchial position. The transactions, positive or negative, are marked by an unnatural power structure and one which has the sanction of the most powerful individuals in the system, the (true) parents.

Both the family and the educational systems reinforce children's perceptions of skewed female superiority and the concommitment male inferiority. In most families, it is the mother who has the primary responsibility for child rearing. This places mothers, females, in the most intimate contact with male and female children and infuses the message that females are powerful and have (almost total) control of them. This gives girls the message that they, because of their gender, enjoy this position of power over boys and that this is a birthright. Boy children experience the condition of always being under the controlling force of a female and to them it is an entirely natural state, one which gets continually reinforced with every transaction between their mothers and themselves.

The powerful mother is joined by other controlling females, the teachers. Especially in the early years of school, positions of authority are occupied by women. Both boys and girls are subject to experiential learning in the classroom which teaches them that, once again, females are in control, nurturing, disciplining, instructing, criticizing, and caring for males. Even when these actions are consistent, reality based, and appropriate to the context, the relationship message that is learned is that females are in a position of superiority to males. In order to survive in such a system, males must learn to respect or tolerate female dominance. Females learn that life continues to be structured so that their gender is the source of benevolent and critical authority.

This picture, however, is not the only one recorded in the minds of children. Everywhere in the lives of both male and female children is another view of dominance and authority which is superimposed on the primary picture. In the wider systems found in society there is much evidence of male supremacy. Power in the corporate, political, religious, and financial worlds is most held by males. Government bodies are generally headed by men; Popes, Bishops, Cardinals, and Priests are men and 'fathers.' The lead character of most mythical, religious, and common folk tales, from Zeus to "Papa Bear," Jesus or Robin Hood were male. However in the field of mythology, religion and fable, females are nearby, i.e., Hera, Mary, Maid Marion.

Within the family system are found pressures to present, preserve, or create a patriarchal style or the facade of such a structure. Some ethnic groups maintain the stance of father as master at all costs while underneath the surface a discerning eye can see that it is the mother, or another strong female, who truly runs the family. There is, in many families, a strong and pervasive covert rule which demands the collusion between the adult male and female to present the man as dominant. This leads to confusion among the children because they are bombarded with messages. At the very minimum sons and daughters are both confused about who they are and who they might become in intimate relationships with the opposite gender. Involving power inside the family system they experience superficial male dominance which is under the covert rigid control of the female. This is followed by more conflicting input from wider systems. Children learn that females can and do dominate boys and yet, at the same time, society and men conspire to maintain women as dependent and weak. The personal ambivalence about the assumption of power and the possible consequences of exerting control has the potential to erode intimate relationships in the adult lives of these impressionable children.

Perhaps in an attempt to maintain congruence and to avoid dissonance, many females adopt the stance that men are naturally superior. They do so both out of needing a sense of consistency and from the pattern which was established by their birth order and family constellation. Girls who adopt this stance, usually identified their mothers as being in a similar position relevant to male authority as they themselves were. They experienced special favors, considerations, and hardships in their roles as subordinates to men. They lived with women doing men's bidding; a mother who depended on her husband for all tangible support and emotional fulfillment. Growing up in this style of system, the daughters adopted the position of males as superior as a way to belong to their system and as a means to gain approval from more favored and powerful figures. As adults these women generally hold the following concepts:

1. Females are dependent on males to do heavy chores and outside tasks.
2. Praise or criticism from men is more serious than that from women.

3. Protection from physical or emotional harm is a duty men perform.
4. All important decisions must have a male's input.
5. Men are more masterful and courageous than women.
6. Men should be in leadership positions in business, government, religion, because they are men.
7. Men in nurturing professions are not masculine.
8. Men are generally more capable than women.
9. Women should be the recipients of men's caretaking.

In addition, women who use this point of view as their reference point, are reluctant to see women in leadership positions. They are non-supportive of equal rights efforts, and they tend to feel uncomfortable with female physicians, psychotherapists, religious leaders, and dislike women being in traditional 'masculine' occupations. This position naturally shapes their mate choice and their careers. They are most comfortable and secure with intimate and other relationships where a man is clearly in the executive hierarchy.

MARITAL SYSTEM FACTORS

The idea of peer interactions is basic to the foundation of intimacy in marriage. Phyllis Rose (1984, p. 93) states that marriages deteriorate "not when love fades . . . but when understanding about the balance of power breaks down, when the weaker member feels exploited or the stronger feels unrewarded for his or her strength." Skewed power relationships such as these described by Rose are clearly disturbances in peer interactions. The two most intense emotional involvements in an intimate relationship are those which involve sex and conflict. Engaging in these two activities in anything other than a state of equality would tend to result in serious impairments which, if rigidly maintained, would eventually lead to the destruction of the relationship. Nevertheless the pressure from past patterns and the anxiety resulting from operating in unfamiliar territory, contributes to the difficulty in maintaining peer interactions.

Inherently, the female models her mode of interaction from her family. In that context she learned to perform tasks from one of three positions; superior, subordinate, or peer. It is possible to carry out any routine couple system from any of these three ego states. Cooking a meal, paying bills, cleaning, going on vacation, or any other task and activity which has a function in the broad couple system can be undertaken from a position of a parent, a servant, or a partner. When a woman presents a meal, does laundry, or engages in intercourse for the exclusive purpose of placating, pampering, or offering solace to her partner, she does so from a position of superiority. If it is undertaken because it is the male's right to expect it, or he is due the favor from her, then she is operating from a position of inferiority. It is a peer activity when each performs tasks because they are chosen, when it gives pleasure, or because it is a part of a quid pro quo agreement between the partners.

When complimentary patterns are established within a marriage, the relationship takes on other parent/child aspects. Since marriage is a system, the mold cannot be set without the explicit cooperation of both partners. Males too have learned to interact with females in prescribed ways. In many cases men fit into a female's theme because they have learned to expect to be treated as if they are a favored son. When he does so, he encourages his wife to mother him, to provide for him all that his 'real' mother could not do or would not do. He attempts to structure the marriage toward a context where he is the ideal son with the ideal mother who embodies eroticism thereby moving sex from a peer activity into the realm of parent child interactions. The existential dilemma erupts when the male does get exactly what he wants: wife as erotic mother, who has sex with him within the boundaries set down by society. He then is apt to discover that the incest taboo may be operating without awareness either within himself, his wife, or both, and this seriously disturbs both partners' ability to engage in physical intimacy as sexual interactions become dysfunctional.

Rose examines this interactional pattern and concludes that there is a "patriarchal paradigm" which enforces men's power in a marriage and spawns "the pilot of female power by weakness" (page 104). This occurs as men work to make themselves worthy of a woman. This is followed by a marriage where he is the executive of the system, she serves him, works to please him, and obtains his protection in return. This is made possible by the woman who, having been wounded by her own family system, believes she needs to be cared for and 'requires an offering of guilt' (Rose 1984).

There is some disagreement about the position of the dominant male in the assessment of the marital interaction. The differences in discrimination may be more a function of the background of the individual completing the assessment than in the reality of the situation. The assessment is more accurately determined by examining the attitude and behavior of the female in the marital system. The male is either operating from a position of critical, domineering father to a dependent daughter, or he is behaving from a tyrannical child state toward his (martyred) mother. He cannot maintain either of these two positions without compliance from his partner. Her responses and reactions are both governed by and encouraging of a static posture.

The complementarity of this set of behaviors must be taken into account. Neither husband nor wife can continue the behavior without the other. The process of blaming or looking for a cause-effect motivator generally leads to the families of origin, and beyond that to ancestry where the determinants are cultural factors, historical context and sociological forces. The importance of identifying the reciprocal composition of the disturbed interaction remains primary. When there are disturbances of intimacy, including sex and conflict, the underlying non-peer interactional pattern should become the reference point for all intervention strategies.

THERAPEUTIC CONSIDERATIONS

There is apt to be a tangential appendage to the non-peer marital system. The clinician should keep in mind the self regulating property of systems. For every action there is an equal and opposite reaction. Therefore, if the present is taken as an arbitrary starting point, the skewed peer interaction may be seen as a reaction to an earlier transaction in a similar or isomorphic dyad. In understanding this property, it is important to become familiar with broader systems in the lives of the couple. The domineering male may be exhibiting behaviors with his wife which were denied to him by his mother. His emotional dependence on his mother may be being expressed by encouraging his wife to be dependent on him. In other words, what mother did to son, son as husband, may attempt wife to do with him. There are also variations to this theme while remaining with the boundaries of the theorems of systems. A husband may interact with his wife in a continuation of his old patterns. He may then extend his equal-and-opposite reaction to his children. To illustrate this concept the example of a perpetual 'son' can be used. What is esoterically referred to as a 'mama's boy', marries a woman who needs someone to mother. She consistently treats him as if he were helpless; choosing his clothing, feeding him, cleaning up after him, and generally keeping him from being able to care for himself. She would be apt to make all major decisions or give her opinions in such a manner that the superficial observer might think he had the major control over decision making, but in reality her input would be able to tip the balance in any direction she decided it should take. The wife would be likely to maintain power and control, either overtly or covertly. The discerning listener might detect a significant note of pride in her complaint that she 'has to do everything for him.' When children enter this rigid system, it is as if the husband takes on the position of a privileged older brother to the children; a parental child. The wife may interact with what she identifies as her family as if her husband were one of the children. Frequently the husband refers to his wife as "Mommy." There is a significant difference in the statements "Do what your Mother says." and "Do what Mommy says." The use of emotionally charged language is generally an indicator of a transactional pattern. "Mommy" repeatedly used, implies a behavioral interaction consistent with the emotions governing the relationship.

The husband in this example has continued the mother-son pattern of his childhood and most likely is following a prescribed pattern of behavior for males and females which is a legacy from his ancestry. The equal-opposite principle may be operating in his manner of interacting with his children. If this is true, he could be a tyrant with them; demanding obedience; meting out harsh discipline and imposing unrealistic expectations. In extreme cases he could be an abuser, either physically or sexually. His inherited rules for interacting with females include the polarities, superior or subordinate, and his intimate relationships include only individuals who have a homologous set of rules.

The risk of abuse to the children increases with the rigidity of the behavioral pattern. When an adult is a regular member of the sibling sub-system in the family it is as if the adult is a peer to the child or children. The adult, unable to complete appropriate adult behaviors within the adult system of peers, then is driven to meet these needs within another system of (perceived) peers, the child system. Appropriate peer behaviors are those involving sex and conflict. When this is not transacted within the adult system, it is often enacted within the child system between an adult and a child (or children) as if they are peers. A fully functioning adult, someone emotionally mature and responsible, would not engage in harmful behavior with a child. It can be assumed that whenever a biological adult is in a consistently rigid inappropriate interaction with a child, the adult is an emotional peer to the child. The adult is operating from a set of behaviors which are arrested at an emotional developmental level which leads him to interact as if he is a peer to a child.

If the equal-opposite principle does not manifest itself within the family system, it then would be evident in the occupational systems. The meek, dependent husband, is often the dictator on the job. The degree of intergenerational contamination is matched by an inappropriately rigid maintenance of hierarchical boundaries. All members of the system find outlets for the expressions denied in primary interactions. Furthermore, the search for cross gender peer seems to continue without end. When it is impossible, or unlikely to take place within one sub-system, it will then be almost compulsively sought after in another sub-system. The wife who has married and maintained her self as 'mother' to her son/husband, will yearn for cross gender peer interactions and perhaps find them in an extra-marital affair where she and her lover are 'equals.'

It is also possible to look at social injustices within this framework. If the basic hypotheses are maintained, then women's repression by men in society might be seen as a reaction to men's historic suppression by females in the narrower system or exactly the reverse. Most uprisings occur when a group feels suppressed.

The struggle to "get even" is basic to all conflict involving a high degree of emotionality. The need to "get even" does not exist between peers. They are emotional equals and enjoy an overall evenness. Getting even exists when one person in a partner system feels one-down, unequal to the other. The motivation to get revenge, another form of getting even, is an inappropriate expression of inequality which actually maintains the emotional inequity. Keeping score, couples fail to realize that a tie represents success. Instead they forego getting even in favor of amassing more 'points,' winning. There is a substantial advantage in assisting a couple to attain or maintain an even status. The danger is, left to themselves, individuals will instead attempt to one-up the partner.

An illustration of this concept can be found in the case of a young couple who sought therapy a few weeks after their marriage. Their presenting problem was that the husband had revealed to his wife, on their wedding day, during the celebration, that he had been having an intense sexual relationship with a woman who was a member of their circle of friends (and who incidentally was a guest at their wedding.) The new wife was devastated. The foundations of her trust in her partner were shaken, and she was not at all confident that the broken covenant could be mended. She was appropriately angry and sad, and felt and acted betrayed. He, on the other hand, more casually dismissed his 'transgression' and staunchly maintained that she should put this all behind them and get the marriage off to a good start. His naivete was astounding. First the therapist facilitated the wife's expression of hurt and anger; realizing that this resulted in a therapeutic impasse, another tact was taken. It became apparent that the couple's relationship had solidified into a transactional pattern which included only a 'naughty son' and a 'scolding mother' or a penitent child begging forgiveness from a saint. The therapist proposed to the couple that it appeared as if their relationship was doomed to deteriorate unless one of two changes were made. The couple was requested to discover means by which either the husband could become as moral and righteous as his wife, or she could join him on his level. The injunction was for the couple to become even, to be peers. The couple responded with surprise and understanding. They conveyed their awareness of the pattern by describing the mother/son relationship and went on to say that this probably was part of the reason why their sex life had suffered. In addition, one of their first responses was that she had considered having an affair to get revenge and he had supported her. The wife claimed, however, that this seemed like she was punishing her husband which also felt like a mother action and therefore she said that although they somehow knew what needed to be done, they were unable to find a solution. They continued to struggle to reclaim their ability to be peers. The hierarchical structure of their relationship continued to be the focus of treatment until they decided that their marriage was a mistake on both of their parts, each accepting a portion of the responsibility for creating a non-workable relationship. They ended their marriage as non-intimate peers.

CONCLUSION

Peers have a high degree of genuine respect for each other. At times they are able to put their own needs aside for the other with the assurance that the same will be done for them. They can be children together which assures that they can have good sex together, that they have the capacity to fight fairly and productively for change, and that they can have fun, play together. As adults, when required, they make decisions for the mutual good of their relationship and for themselves knowing that the 'Me' impacts on the 'We.' Also, they can nurture each other and themselves appropriately since they have the capacity to parent. Fully functional peer ability provides the basis for an increasing capacity for intimacy and therefore a viable rich marriage.

There is both a challenge and a difficulty associated with adopting the Peer Principle in working with couples in therapy. When the therapist embraces this concept as central to the solidarity of the relationship, it must become an enforceable position which will permeate every action, transaction, and intervention. The difficulty becomes evident in determining the hierarchical position of the therapist relative to the couple. In working toward the goal of fostering peer interactions, does the therapist encourage the couple to be co-children, siblings, in response to the therapist-as-parent? Should the couple become co-parents if the therapist adopts (therapeutically) an inept child position? Or should the therapeutic trio become a peer group where the boundaries between client and therapist are apt to be subject to diffusion? While a definitive answer may impossible, the issue of therapist power and the nature of equality will require attention if the integrity of treatment is to be maintained relative to the properties of isomorphic processes.

Further, the therapist who recognizes the need to restructure the power balance in the marriage must be flexible enough to use the couple's content and process as the vehicle for change. This can be infinitely more complex than a direct approach utilizing advice, tasks, and insights. The multi-dimensional nature of power, a recognition of all the subterfuges of power, and a familiarity with the therapist's personal issues with power, especially as they are gender biased, are weighty and imperative therapist prerequisites for success.

Every interaction has nuances of power in the process of transaction. Every interaction in the therapeutic setting has to be assessed, noted, and guided with attention to this function. When this occurs, the therapist effectively restructures the marital balance resulting in a union which leaves the individuals better equipped to deal with the resolution of their problems and the pursuit of happiness without the interference of a therapist.

REFERENCES

Berne, E. (1961). *Transactional analysis in psychotherapy.* New York: Grove Press.

Sex in Human Loving. (1970). New York: Simon & Schuster.

Horewitz, J.S. (1981). *Family therapy and transactional analysis.* New York: Jason Aronson.

Rose, P. (1984). *Parallel lives: Five victorian marriages.* New York: Vintage Books.

Empowerment Themes
for Couples Therapy

Judith Bula Jacobs

SUMMARY. Empowerment is defined as a process occurring in a relational context in which all participants in the relationship interact in a manner which establishes connection and strengthens each person's sense of self worth and personal power. The purpose of the article is to apply specific themes of empowerment for couples therapy. Six major themes are presented: (1) taking and being in charge of one's self; (2) acknowledging and valuing difference and diversity; (3) power in relationship; (4) choices and options; (5) necessity of skills in relating to the wider societal context; and (6) taking action. Techniques for working with couples from an empowerment perspective are also offered.

INTRODUCTION

In recent years, the term "empowerment" has rapidly become a familiar word. It has been used in personal, interpersonal, organizational, and political contexts. It has been found applicable in multiple professional disciplines from business to human services. It has been defined as a goal, a strategy, a process, a state-of-being, a program, an intervention, an approach, and a world view. The roots of empowerment theory can be found in the human rights movement, political psychology, feminist theory, community organization principles, and "andragogy," the facilitating of adult learning. The specific use of the themes of empowerment in the context of couples therapy has yet to be addressed. This is the purpose of this present article.

Judith B. Jacobs, PhD, is Assistant Professor, University of Denver Graduate School of Social Work, Denver, CO 80208.

This expansive usefulness of empowerment attests to its universality but it can also mean that it gets used in ambiguous, confusing and vague ways. The first discussion below will, therefore, present some of the definitions of empowerment currently being used in the literature and will clearly define how the term is being used here. Second, several major empowerment themes which appear repeatedly in the literature will be highlighted and discussed, focusing specifically on their relevance to couples and couples therapy. Third, a closer look at some techniques for working with couples from an empowerment perspective will be offered. This will include consideration of the empowering helping relationship as well as specific empowering techniques. Finally, thinking will be directed toward the future and some of the next steps for theory, practice, research, and education of the empowerment perspective for couples therapy.

EMPOWERMENT DEFINED

According to Gutierrez (1990), empowerment is "a process of increasing personal, interpersonal, or political power so that individuals can take action to improve their life situations." (p. 149) She describes the use of the term by macro level authors (i.e., Fagan, 1979; O'Connell, 1978) "as the process of increasing collective political power" and other uses by micro level authors (i.e., Pernell, 1985; Pinderhughes, 1983; Sherman and Wenocur, 1983; Simmons and Parsons, 1983a, 1983b) as "the development of a personal feeling of increased power or control without an actual change in structural arrangements" (p. 150). Gutierrez, however, writes from still a third perspective promoted by authors who are addressing the interface of the two definitions above (i.e., Bock, 1980; Gould, 1987a, 1987b; Kieffer, 1984; Longres and McLeod, 1980; Morell, 1987; Schechter, Szymanski, and Cahill, 1985). This third perspective . . .

. . . suggests a sense of control over one's life in personality, cognition, and motivation. It expresses itself at the level of feelings, at the level of ideas about self worth, at the level of being able to make a difference in the world around us. (Rappaport, 1985, p. 17)

For couples therapy, this definition addresses the important aspect of empowering each of the individuals in the dyad and the personal sense of empowerment on the part of the therapist. It does not, however, address the equally important aspect of empowering the interpersonal nature of the couple's relationship and the interpersonal nature of the therapeutic relationship between the couple and the therapist. For such a definition, we can turn to Janet Surrey (1987), who defines empowerment as:

> . . . the motivation, freedom and capacity to act purposefully, with the mobilization of the energies, resources, strengths, or powers of each person through a mutual, relational process. Personal empowerment can be viewed only through connection, i.e., through the establishment of mutually empathic and mutually empowering relationships. Thus, personal empowerment and the relational context through which this emerges must always be considered simultaneously. (p. 3)

Whereas, the earlier definition of Rappaport is presented more in terms of a personal goal or product, Surrey's definition makes clear the relational process nature of empowerment. There is a constant, dynamic, ever-changing transaction which defines the context of both personal and interpersonal empowerment as well as in the wider political and social arenas. Relationship is primary in Surrey's views of the empowerment process.

> The alternative model of interaction that we are proposing might be termed 'power *with*' or 'power *together*' or 'power emerging from *interaction*' model. It . . . (suggests) that all participants in the relationship interact in ways that build connection and enhance everyone's personal power. (1987, p. 4) What is required is a recognition that relationships are the source of power and effectiveness, not of weakness or inaction or a threat to effectiveness. (1987, p. 9)

Thus, the relationship between the two members of a couple and the relationship between these individuals and the therapist or cotherapists is a primary focus for understanding the nature of empowerment in the practice situation. Part of that nature which cannot be overlooked is the discrepancy which exists in the actual and/

or perceived power on the part of clients and practitioners. With relevance especially in attitudes toward women, the work of Burden and Gottlieb (1987) is helpful:

> Since social work practice at its best is a process of client empowerment, attitudes toward women clients which prevent empowerment are particularly important to observe. Attitudes which stereotype women according to traditional sex-role biases are likely to maintain them in their dependent patient/ client role and prevent them from achieving independent power. (p. 2)

Supporting these words of caution about the importance of attending to potential bias which may disempower women, the author wishes to emphasize additional attitudinal categories relevant to practice with couples. First, attitudes which stereotype men according to traditional sex-role biases may also serve as a barrier toward their achievement of personal power. Secondly, attitudes which stereotype lesbian and gay couples can result in a similar barrier. Further, attitudes stereotyping interracial or crosscultural couples; couples not fitting the age norm, i.e., with more than a ten year span in their ages or older women and younger men couples; couples without children; unmarried couples; and couples living in different cities, states, or countries must be examined. The specific tasks of any helping professional working with couples include gaining accurate information to aid in separating stereotype from fact, examining one's own personal values and making responsible decisions from them, and being clearly aware of one's degrees of acceptance or nonacceptance of those who choose lifestyles different from the norm, striving toward greater acceptance of diversity. "Through our diversity we find our strengths" (Katz, 1988, p. 3). A diverse society, such as the one of which we are a part,

> . . . must be built on strength, not weakness; on contribution, not limitation; on opportunity, not deficiency. A society built on deficit, weakness and limitation finds itself in collapse. A society built on strength, contribution, and opportunity is empowered. (Katz, 1988, p. 3)

Likewise, in the great diversity of definitions for empowerment is also the strength of this concept for enhancing our understanding about its use for couples therapy. For example, the above definitions together address self, other, and context— empowerment of individuals, empowerment in relationship, and factors of an empowered society. For a focus on couples this allows attention on both the subsystems (the individuals) in the couple as well as the societal suprasystem. Such an holistic perspective is essential in comprehending the complexity of issues faced by couples who seek therapeutic services.

Drawing from these various contributions, the definition of empowerment which will be used for this article is: Empowerment is a process occurring in a relational context in which all participants in the relationship interact in a manner which establishes connection and strengthens each person's sense of self worth and personal power.

MAJOR THEMES OF EMPOWERMENT

Several interrelated themes emerge from an overview of the literature on empowerment: (1) taking and being in charge of one's self; (2) acknowledging and valuing difference and diversity; (3) power in relationships; (4) choices and options; (5) necessity of skills in relating to the wider social context; and (6) taking action. Each will be described with special emphasis on relevance to couples therapy.

Taking and Being in Charge of One's Self

Couples often enter therapy with the sense that people other than themselves are in charge of their lives, their choices, their decision-making. It is not unusual to hear and observe the feelings of powerlessness which accompany this sense. Accusations may be directed toward the other partner, members of the extended family, or the work situation. As long as the locus of control is "out there," the possibilities for change appear remote. When that locus is returned to the individual, being able to do something about one's situation becomes much more attainable.

The fundamental empowering transformation . . . is in the transition from sense of self as helpless victim to sense of self as assertive and efficacious citizen. Achieving empowerment also implies developing the skills and resources needed to confront the root sources which create and perpetuate victimization. (Kieffer, 1984, p. 32)

All that is done in the therapeutic relationship to enable each member of the couple to take and be in charge of self strengthens the couple as a whole. This includes the therapist's taking and being in charge of self also and the powerful experiential example this provides for the couple.

Acknowledging and Valuing Difference and Diversity

"The chances of spouses having things in common are about 100 percent. Likewise the chances are 100 percent that they will find differences from one another" (Satir, 1988, pp. 146-7). Observing the similarities and the differences in couples is an important step in assessment of the relationship but seeing what they do with them, especially with their differences, is significant for empowerment.

Couples often bring with them a myth about differences which needs dispelling before any efforts toward empowerment can take place. This myth appears in various forms with the theme: When you agree with me — i.e., when we are the same — then you love me and when you disagree with me — i.e. when we are different — then you do not love me. Differences are often feared because they are seen as leading to conflict. To avoid conflict is a strong message carried by many so this may, in turn, mean avoid differences.

Empowering messages, however, acknowledge both a destructive and constructive use of differences. When we use our differences in constructive ways, they can lead to greater understanding and closeness for the couple. One result can be a greater appreciation for the uniqueness of the other, the self, and the relationship. "Diversity is seen as . . . strength, allowing each person to be a full contributing member of the system" (Katz, 1988, p. 30). When each member is contributing fully, conflict is going to be inevitable as part of the health of the relationship. A couple committed to empowerment has learned to make their conflict, their differences, work for them rather than against them.

Power in Relationships

From the empowerment perspective, "Power is seen as a shared, expandable and renewable resource. Relationships, therefore, are characterized as horizontal in nature, participatory, cooperative, caring, collaborative, and reciprocal" (Lazzari, 1990, p. 17).

Couples in difficulty are often functioning from an hierarchical stance with each other rather than from one which is horizontal. Patterns of dominance and submission perpetuate competitive interactions rather than ones which are cooperative and reciprocal. Power is viewed as "power over" rather than "empowerment with."

When couples bring hierarchical and competitive mind sets with them into the context of therapy, they may expect that similar uses of power will be seen in the therapist-to-client relationship also. It is, therefore, crucial for the therapist to once again recognize the power of modeling which can occur as she or he works to create an environment for the couple which can truly be empowering both by what is said as well as by what is done.

An absence of hierarchical relationships which are disempowering for members in a system does not mean an absence of structure in the relationships between them. Structure is defined in terms of roles which carry a variety of related tasks. These roles and tasks are recognized as different, all being necessary for the growthful functioning of the whole system, but the roles and tasks do not get labeled in "better than/worse than" or "more/less" terms which are part of hierarchical thinking and action.

Choices and Options

One of the most empowering actions available to therapists, whether working with individuals or couples or families or larger systems, is that of helping the client recognize as many choices as possible in each situation. When clients speak to us in terms such as, "There is no other choice, this is the only one we have," they are conveying a sense of feeling trapped and powerless to make a difference in their lives. Similarly, when they communicate only two choices, this portrays the helplessness of an either/or dilemma, with both of the choices usually feeling equally inadequate. It is the either-or which is most often present in couple dynamics when the power struggle has become a predominant mode of interaction for them.

The empowerment perspective emphasizes the necessity of considering multiple choices and options. It encourages a "both-and-and-and . . ." view of alternatives rather than the either/or view. A greater sense of creativity, possibility, and freedom often gets expressed by couples as they see the expansiveness of options rather than what may have seemed restrictive earlier.

> Choices and options must be developed. This assumes a view of people as knowing what is best for them and as being able to make independent decisions. Personal realities are validated. Individual strengths and capabilities are operationalized through the value of self-determination. (Lazzari, 1990, p. 17)

Necessity of Skills in Relating to the Wider Social Context

Arriving at a sense of individual and couple empowerment within the partnership is a highly significant step for any couple who has previously experienced the frustration and pain of a disempowering relationship. This accomplishment runs the risk of being undermined, however, if couples do not also possess skills in connecting their individual situations with the wider social context which has an ongoing impact on the nature and quality of their relationship. This is a reality for all couples but especially for those couples whose lifestyles differ from the cultural norms.

We live in a culture which has established a set of norms for coupling: heterosexual coupling, coupling within one's race and ethnic group, coupling which observes certain rules about age difference between the two people. Gay and lesbian couples, interracial and cross-cultural couples and couples whose ages do not fit the patterns of the norm, i.e., with more than a ten year span in their ages or the older woman—younger man couples, are constantly confronted with actual or potential prejudicial and discriminatory behaviors against them. Couples therapists choosing to work from an empowerment perspective validate the diversity of lifestyles available to couples and they keep themselves accurately informed about the realities and challenges being faced by those of the various lifestyles so as not to perpetuate disempowering myths and biases. Furlong (1987) has stated that empowerment of clients is not likely to occur unless "structural influences" including gender, ethnicity, and class are considered as integral parts of the problems presented by clients.

Differences in lifestyle are likely to be present in the therapeutic relationship between therapist and clients. The clinical situation provides the opportunity for experiencing the difference within the empowerment perspective through valuing the uniqueness of each individual and acknowledging the strengths in our diversity. Translating this experience into the wider social context of the couple — i.e., their respective work situations, their families, their participation in organizations, the social policies which address or ignore their needs — is a crucial aspect in acting from the empowerment perspective.

Taking Action

Taking action to meet one's needs and participation with others who share a common purpose is encouraged. This action contributes to empowering relationships and to an empowering community for all persons involved (Fabricant, 1988; Katz, 1984; Kieffer, 1984; Lazzari, 1990; Zimmerman, 1986). It is in action that the felt sense of empowerment becomes visible.

In the therapeutic situation with couples, no experience of therapy will be complete if empowerment is left as simply another possible way to perceive the relationship. Words and actions hold equal importance. The language of empowerment can be fostered in the couple's communication patterns as well as the behaviors which convey the cooperation and caring which are characteristic when empowering each other is a priority.

Likewise, the therapist cannot simply talk about the importance of or the need for empowerment. From the moments of initial greeting to the ending of the therapeutic relationship, modeling the thought, speech and action of the empowerment perspective provides congruence between what is said and what the accompanying actions exemplify. Some of the specifics of working with couples from this perspective are the subjects of the next section.

WORKING WITH COUPLES
FROM AN EMPOWERMENT PERSPECTIVE

When committed to using an empowerment perspective in clinical practice, therapists are aware that this perspective comes alive in the nature of the relationship between clients and therapist as much as it does in specific techniques which can be used to promote empowerment themes. Indeed, without the supporting context of an empowering relationship, any technique used runs the risk of being shallow and "techniquey." The following discussion, therefore, focuses first on necessary factors in the empowering helping relationship and, secondly, on specific empowering techniques.

The Empowering Helping Relationship

The potential for empowering relationships in couples therapy is fourfold when a couple is working with a single therapist: (1) between partner A and therapist; (2) between partner B and therapist; (3) between the couple (A and B as a dyad) and therapist; and (4) between partner A and partner B. (This potential increases to six possibilities when a cotherapist is also present.) As it is the therapist who is primarily responsible for promoting a perspective of empowerment, at least initially, observation of each of these interactions must be ongoing throughout the therapeutic process. Empowerment in any one of these interactions has an influence on the occurrence of empowerment in all of the others and in the creating and maintaining of the overall helping environment.

The centrality of the relationship in the empowerment process is emphasized by a variety of authors (Furlong, 1987; Ingram, 1988; Shapiro, 1983; Weick, 1983). The quality of this relationship, in order to be empowering, has also been found to include certain characteristics of the helper: one who conveys her or his own sense of personal empowerment (Brandwein, 1987; Reisch, Wenocur, and Sherman, 1981; Sherman and Wenocur, 1983); one whose "focus is on strengths, not deficits, and on the potential for growth and needed . . . change" (Germain and Gitterman, 1987, p. 496); one who "assumes that people can direct their own destinies" (Hegar and Hunzeker, 1988, p. 501); one who is personally compatible, supportive and able to empathize with feelings, respectful of ideas and feelings that may differ from the therapist's, and open about own feelings (Marshall, 1982, pp. 224-225).

Basing her observations on the works of Bock (1980), Fagan (1979), Keefe (1980), Pinderhughes (1983), Schechter et al. (1985), and Solomon (1976), Gutierrez captures a summary of ideas about the empowering helping relationship:

> The basis of empowering practice is a helping relationship based on collaboration, trust, and the sharing of power. To avoid replicating the powerlessness that the client experiences with other helpers or professionals, it is critical that the worker perceive himself or herself as an enabler, organizer, a consultant, or a compatriot with the client. The interaction between worker and client should be characterized by genuineness, mutual respect, open communication, and informality. It presumes that the worker does not hold the answers to the client's problems, but rather that in the context of collaboration, the client will develop the insights, skills, and capacity to resolve the situation. (Gutierrez, 1990, p. 151)

Empowering Techniques

In addition to the nature of the empowering relationship, it is also noted that certain patterns of communication, certain modalities for empowering practice, and specific techniques have been suggested.

Patterns of communication which are most commonly seen in empowering helping relationships are those which are symmetrical, where the persons are "essentially peers with fairly equal likelihood of having power, initiating tasks, or otherwise guiding the directions which role functioning might take" (Nelsen, 1974, p. 237).

Somers (1971) offers suggestions for maintaining the symmetry, or the shared power, which include discussing alternatives, collaborating, and providing choices and shared decision-making in matters of mutual concern.

Maintaining symmetrical communication in couples therapy can be one of the most distinct challenges for the couples therapist. A frequent observation with couples who seek therapy is a noticeable lack of symmetry, or balance, in the quantity and quality of their communication. A couple in a competitive mode will vie for equal "air time" with the therapist. For partners who have a dominant-submissive pattern, one may do nearly all the talking while the other sits silently. It has been suggested that the therapist must not allow more than three to four exchanges from one partner before turning to the other partner for input or feedback in order to maintain a symmetrical balance in the communication (Broderick, 1983).

Working from an empowerment perspective is applicable in all modalities. Whether with individuals, couples, families, at the community level or beyond, an empowering helping relationship and its accompanying techniques can have a significant impact. There is one modality, however, which shows up more frequently than the others as being most effective for empowering interventions. It is the modality of the small group.

> It (small group work) can be the perfect environment for raising consciousness, engaging in mutual aid, developing skills, and solving problems and an ideal way for clients to experience individual effectiveness in influencing others. (Guiterrez, 1990, p. 151)

Couples group therapy is supported as a highly effective modality for promoting awareness about empowering relationships. The experiential nature of one couple observing and participating with empowering actions of their therapist has been emphasized earlier. The group situation allows for the power of this type of learning to increase to a significant degree by nature of the multiple couples and their variety of interactions.

Finally, a helpful repertoire of specific empowering techniques can be found in the literature. All can apply to practice with couples.

- create a climate of acceptance not because it is the right thing to do but because it creates the enabling of both partners to be more effective; treat client's perceptions as real; foster commitment to action; provide multiple opportunities for change; emphasize the power individuals have to create change; stay on course; redefine the relationship as a support system; see issues as processes, not products (Katz, 1988, pp. 36-47).
- celebrate successes and changes; do not lose sight of the positive changes (Shepard, 1985, p. 4).
- maintain a commitment to mutuality throughout all stages of the helping process; frequently indicate an appreciation of the client's areas and level of competency; acknowledge strengths; nurture self-exploration; be supportive of each person's role as a valuable contributor to the relationship (Lazzari, 1990, pp. 92-113).
- accept the client's definition of the problem; identify and build upon existing strengths; engage in a power analysis of the client's situation; teach specific skills; mobilize resources and advocate for clients (Gutierrez, 1990, pp. 151-152).

All of these techniques help to shape the empowering environment for therapeutic work with couples. The task is not complete, however, if attention is not also given to the ways in which couples can translate their experiences of empowerment in the therapeutic situation to their personal and social situations outside therapy. In order to take this next step, couples will benefit from the technique of stepping outside of their current experience and imagining, or envisioning, what kind of relationship they want to have. In Peter Block's (1987) words: "We become empowered when we create around ourselves a bubble that expresses our wishes of what we want to create" (p. 190). Enabling new images, new visions, of what a couple is yet to become to be a part of the therapeutic process allows for an anticipation of the future of their relationship beyond the repetition of earlier struggles. Instead, that anticipation from the empowerment perspective is based on their own hopes and their own awareness of multiple opportunities.

CONCLUSION

Next steps are evident for advancing our clinical understanding of empowerment theory for couples therapy. Some of the areas for future inquiry in the theory of the empowerment perspective for couples include the steps a couple experiences when making a transition from traditional role definitions to ones which are more empowering of the individuals and ways in which an empowerment stance in the marital dyad translates into parenting tasks.

For practice, further inquiry into the ways in which professionals insure their own senses of empowerment within an agency or private practice situation could enhance the capacity for their being able to present an empowered self with clients. The modeling role itself could also use further attention in the couples therapy literature.

Helpful research could include study of couples who are found to be naturally empowering of each other. Asking what factors are essential in the transition from a disempowering relationship to an empowering one could also be an important area for research.

Lastly, the empowerment perspective needs to be taught as it relates to practice with couples. Academic settings and supervisory contexts can benefit from empowering relationships between educators and students, supervisors and supervisees, and from the use of empowering techniques.

REFERENCES

Block, P. (1987). *The empowered manager.* San Francisco: Jossey-Bass.

Bock, S. (1982). Conscientization: Paolo Friere and class-based practice. *Catalyst, 2,* 5-25.

Brandwein, R. (1987). Women in macro practice. In *Encyclopedia of social work* (18th ed., Vol. 2, pp. 881-892). Silver Spring, MD: National Association of Social Workers.

Broderick, C. (1983). *The therapeutic triangle: A sourcebook on marital therapy.* Beverly Hills: Sage.

Burden, D., and Gottlieb, N. (Eds.). (1987). *The woman client.* New York: Tavistock.

Fabricant, M. (1988). Empowering the homeless. *Social Policy, 18*(4), 49-55.

Fagan, H. (1979). *Empowerment: Skills for parish social action.* New York: Paulist Press.

Furlong, M. (1987). A rationale for the use of empowerment as a goal in casework. *Australian Social Work, 40*(3), 25-30.

Germain, C. and Gitterman, A. (1987). Ecological Perspective. In *Encyclopedia of social work* (18th ed., Vol. 1, pp. 488-499), Silver Spring, MD: National Association of Social Workers.

Gould, K. (1987a). Feminist principles and minority concerns: Contributions, problems, and solutions. *Affilia: Journal of Women and Social Work, 3,* 6-19.

Gould, K. (1987b). Life model vs. conflict model: A feminist perspective. *Social Work, 32,* 346-351.

Gutierrez, L. (1990). Working with women of color: An empowerment perspective. *Social Work, 35,* 149-153.

Hegar, R., and Hunzeker, J. (1988). Moving toward empowerment-based practice in public child welfare. *Social Work 33*(3), 499-501.

Ingram, R. (1988). Empower. *Social Policy, 19*(2), 11-16.

Katz, J. (1988). Facing the challenge of diversity and multiculturalism. *Working Paper #360,* Center for Research on Social Organization, Ann Arbor: University of Michigan Press.

Katz, R. (1984). Empowerment and synergy: Expanding the community's healing resources. *Prevention in Human Services, 3,* 201-226.

Keefe, T. (1980). Empathy skill and critical consciousness. *Social Casework, 61,* 387-393.

Kieffer, C. (1984). Citizen empowerment: A developmental perspective. In J. Rappaport, C. Swift, and R. Heww (Eds.), *Studies in empowerment: Toward understanding and action* (pp. 9-36). New York: The Haworth Press, Inc.

Lazzari, M. (1990). *Empowerment, gender content, and field education.* Unpublished Doctoral Dissertation, University of Denver Graduate School of Social Work.

Longres, J., and McLeod, E. (1980). Consciousness raising and social work practice. *Social Casework, 61,* 267-277.

Marshall, C. (1982). Social work students' perception of their practicum experience: A study of learning by doing (Doctoral dissertation, The University of Toronto, 1982). *Dissertation Abstracts International, 44,* 645-A.

Morell, C. (1987). Cause is function: Toward a feminist model of integration for social work. *Social Service Review, 61,* 144-155.

Nelsen, J. (1974). Relationship communication in early fieldwork conferences. *Social Casework, 55*(4), 237-243.

O'Connell, B. (1978). From service delivery to advocacy to empowerment. *Social Casework, 59,* 195-202.

Pernell, R. (1985). Empowerment and social group work. In M. Parenes (Ed.),

Innovations in social group work: Feedback from practice to theory (pp. 107-117). New York: The Haworth Press, Inc.

Pinderhughes, E. (1983). Empowerments for our clients and for ourselves. *Social Casework, 64,* 331-338.

Rappaport, J. (1985). The power of empowerment language. *Social Policy, 17*(2), 15-21.

Reisch, M., Wenocur, S., and Sherman, W. (1981). Empowerment, conscientization and animation as core social work skills. *Social Development Issues, 5*(2/3), 108-120.

Satir, V. (1988). *The new peoplemaking.* Mountain View, CA: Science and Behavior Books.

Schechter, S., Szymanski, S., and Cahill, M. (1985). *Violence against women: A curriculum for empowerment* (facilitator's manual). New York: Women's Education Institute.

Shapiro, J. (1983). Commitment to disenfranchised clients. In A. Rosenblatt and D. Waldfogel (Eds.), *Handbook of clinical social work* (pp. 888-903). San Francisco: Jossey-Bass.

Shepard, H. (1985). Rules of thumb for change agents. *OD Practitioner, 17*(4), 1-5.

Sherman, W., and Wenocur, S. (1983). Empowering public welfare workers through mutual support. *Social Work, 28,* 375-379.

Simmons, C., and Parsons, R. (1983a). Developing internality and perceived competence: The empowerment of adolescent girls. *Adolescence, 18,* 917-922.

Simmons, C., and Parsons, R. (1983b). Empowerment for role alternatives in adolescence. *Adolescence, 18,* 193-200.

Solomon, B. (1976). *Black empowerment.* New York: Columbia University Press.

Somers, M. (1971) Dimensions and dynamics of engaging the learner. *Journal of Education for Social Work, 7*(3), 49-57.

Surrey, J. (1987). *Relationship and empowerment.* Work in progress #30. Wellesley, MA: Stone Center for Developmental Services and Studies.

Weick, A. (1983). Issues in overturning a medical model of social work practice. *Social Work, 28*(6), 467-471.

Zimmerman, M. (1986). Citizen participation, perceived control, and psychological empowerment (Doctoral dissertation, University of Illinois at Urbana-Champaign, 1986). *Dissertation Abstracts International, 47,* 4335-B

The Co-Construction of New Meanings in Couple Relationships: A Psychoeducational Model That Promotes Mutual Empowerment

Maryhelen Snyder

SUMMARY. The gender informed psychotherapist has the challenge of addressing power issues in couple relationships in a manner that is both gender sensitive and blame free. The Relationship Enhancement model of couple therapy (Guerney, 1977) is particularly suitable for doing this. The model integrates the qualities of empathy and autonomy that are culturally considered feminine and masculine respectively. It systematically teaches couples how to interact with each other in a non-blaming way that is deeply empathic, rationally assertive, and sensitive to how meanings can be both de-constructed and co-constructed in dialogue. The model also permits the integration of relevant techniques from other therapeutic approaches.

Lois and Steven had been living separately for several months when they came for therapy. Steven had initiated the effort to come back together as a couple. He described their decision to separate, which he had actually initiated, as "a tragic mistake." Lois was more cautious than Steve about moving back together; she was enjoying a new-found sense of independence and the power to make decisions for herself. After 4 weeks of therapy, they had established a friendship with each other that felt strong and satisfying, but

Maryhelen Snyder, PhD, is a psychologist in private practice in Albuquerque, NM. She is currently clinical director of the New Mexico Relationship Enhancement Institute, 422 Camino del Bosque NW, Albuquerque, NM 87114.

41

Steven was experiencing increasing frustration that Lois was unwilling to re-engage in a sexual relationship. When he spoke of his frustration about this, he acknowledged that he was angry at her for "not even working on whatever was getting in the way," and he said, "I don't know how much longer I can wait." She responded to this with intense anger, saying that she felt she was back "in the fifties" when men felt they had a right to demand sex of women, and that she simply wasn't going to make love until she felt more trust in the relationship.

This case, which will be described in further detail below, reveals a typical struggle between men and women who are in partner relationships. As the old patriarchal arrangements increasingly break down, new arrangements for which often there are no models need to be constructed. The therapist is a participant-observer in this process. Given the dominant/subordinate relationship of men and women historically (Lerner, 1986; J. Miller, 1976; Okin, 1989), as well as of parents and children (A. Miller, 1981), and different socio-economic and cultural groups, the therapist, both male and female, faces the critical challenge of actively avoiding an unaware re-enactment of hierarchical, patriarchal, adultist, and elitist cultural practices. These practices pervade the field of psychotherapy as strongly as they do any other field. We are taught as therapists to pathologize, examine, diagnose, prescribe, treat, cure, intervene, and evaluate (Luepnitz, 1988). A high level of consciousness and effort is needed to extract ourselves from our culturally embedded beliefs and practices so we may be sensitive participant-observers in the changes in these hierarchical arrangements that are occurring throughout the world.

At the same time the therapist must maintain the natural authority that is consensually bestowed on someone who is trained to be a helper in a particular domain. The therapist is the manager of the dialogue that takes place in the therapy session, and is responsible for structuring it in such a way that healing and problem solving (or dissolving) can take place. In the last several years, I have been using the Relationship Enhancement model of couple therapy (Guerney, 1977; Snyder, 1989, in press-a, in press-b) for the dual reason that it invites my rigorous practice of non-hierarchical and gender-sensitive forms of therapy, and it teaches couples to engage in effective dialogue from a position of equality.

THE MANAGEMENT
OF THE THERAPEUTIC CONVERSATION

In the last decade social constructivists (Anderson and Goolishian, 1988, 1991; Goolishian and Anderson, 1987; Hare-Mustin, 1987; Hoffman, 1990; Maturana and Varela, 1987; White, 1986) have been emphasizing in the last decade that effective therapy must be a type of conscious conversation in which current meanings are de-constructed and new meanings co-constructed by the participants. Anderson and Goolishian (1988) define change as the evolution of new meanings in dialogue. Relationship Enhancement (RE) couple therapy provides an effective structure for managing a co-constructive conversation.

In order for constructive conversations on conflictual topics to take place, there must be a structure for what Gregory Bateson called "double or multiple description" (Bateson, 1972, 1979; White, 1986). Bateson compared this process to binary vision in which the viewpoint of each eye contributes to the three-dimensionality and richness of the whole. The animal impulse in the face of conflict is to protect oneself as all animals do with fighting, fleeing, or yielding. On the human plane these responses involve a large repertoire of deeply conditioned controlling, withdrawing, or complying behaviors (Paul & Paul, 1983). To forego these behaviors and instead to use the tool of language to share viewpoints openly and dialogue toward new meanings usually requires the three elements of: (a) structure for conversation, (b) skill at engaging in conversation, and (c) willingness to engage in such conversation.

RE couple therapy contributes to all three of these conversation requirements. It structures an uninterrupted time for dialogue, the adequate separation of listening and expressing, and guidelines for staying on task. It teaches the skills of empathy, effective expression, discussion, and conflict resolution. By explicitly reinforcing progress as well as permitting the couple to experience the intrinsic satisfaction of constructive conversation, it enhances the couple's willingness to make new choices.

THE HISTORICAL CONTEXT OF GENDER ISSUES

Everywhere one turns these days, historians, sociolinguists, anthropologists, and psychologists are writing about why men and women "just don't understand" each other (Tannen, 1990). In her outstanding historical analysis, *The Creation of Patriarchy,* Gilda Lerner (1986) points out that the structure of patriarchy was co-constructed by man and women because it worked as an adaptation during a certain stage of historical development. Although women have been subordinate in the structure, man did not invent it for the purpose of hurting women. Men have been damaged by it as well, and many man, as they learn more about that damage, are as eager to change the old structures as are women (Napier, 1991).

Nevertheless, among the arrangements that men and women developed and are still deeply embedded in in spite of the slow, painful, and exciting changes that are occurring are:

1. Men as "bread winners," responsible for the family's monetary survival.
2. Men as "warriors," responsible for the family's physical survival.
3. Women as homemakers, responsible for the family's daily well-being.
4. Women as nurturers, responsible for the care of the children and the emotional well-being of the family.
5. Women as the property of man, sexually obligated.
6. Men as the authorities in all social institutions.
7. Women as divided into two types, which is now often experienced as two "selves": The "good" women and wife, obedient, saintly, and asexual; and the "bad" woman, sexual, free of the family's restraints and the family's advantages.
8. Men as the learned ones, responsible for science, philosophy, political and economic analysis.
9. Women as the primary parent of boys, leading frequently to a

marital re-enactment of mother-son dynamics in our culture (Chodorow, 1978; Dinnerstein, 1976).

There is increasingly widespread acknowledgment that the differences between men and women are only minimally biological (even given the likelihood of the genetic effect resulting from the difference in what has been adaptive for men and women), and rather have been constituted culturally in language, belief systems, and practices (Allen and Laird, 1990; Hare-Mustin, 1987; Neal and Slobodnik, 1990). It is critical, however, that this growing awareness not diminish our attention to the harmful nature of many of our current gender constructs. In *Justice, Gender, and the Family,* Susan Moller Okin (1989) discusses the "false gender neutrality" that discounts the reality that our different histories have resulted in radically different conditioning and radically different life circumstances. In her view:

> A just future would be one without gender. In its social structures and practices, one's sex would have no more relevance than one's eye color or the length of one's toes. No assumptions would be made about "male" and "female" roles; childbearing would be so conceptually separated from child rearing and other family responsibilities that it would be a cause for surprise, and no little concern, if men and women were not equally responsible for domestic life or if children were to spend much more time with one parent than the other. It would be a future in which men and women participated in more or less equal numbers in every sphere of life, from infant care to different kinds of paid work to high-level politics. (Okin, 1989, p. 171)

This quietly passionate statement reveals how far we have to go as a culture and how difficult the struggles may be as we co-construct this future together. The therapeutic function is a very critical one in empowering clients to participate consciously and caringly in these changes to whatever degree they are ready to do so. What is needed is a way to concretely operationalize therapeutic empowerment of clients and, in turn, the partner's empowerment of one another in the direction of developing the capacity for co-constructive conversations. Relationship Enhancement couple therapy is one carefully delineated and researched method for doing this.

THE APPLICATIONS
OF RELATIONSHIP ENHANCEMENT
COUPLE THERAPY

RE therapy is a non-diagnostic, non-pathologizing, psycho-educational model. The model has been well researched for over two decades. A meta-analytic study (Giblin, Sprenkle, & Sheehan, 1985) revealed the model to be more effective than either rational-emotive or behavioral exchange models, and to be the only widely known named program that fared better than non-named models of therapy. Other studies have compared the model to the Couples Communication Program (Brock & Joanning, 1983), Jesse's Gestalt Relationship Facilitation Program (Jesse & Guerney, 1981), and various flexible therapeutic approaches of experienced marital and family therapists in a community mental health center (Ross, Baker, & Guerney, 1985). All these studies revealed RE therapy to be significantly more effective than the approaches to which they were compared. The RE model has been effectively applied to highly stressed couples and families and to the treatment of spouse abuse and wife-battering (Waldo, 1987; Guerney, Waldo, & Firestone, 1987; Hardley & Guerney, 1989).

The Central Role of Empathy

In Relationship Enhancement therapy, beginning with the intake interview, each person is listened to carefully and empathized with fully. An attempt is made to grasp the "lifeworld" (Grunebaum, 1990; Habermas, 1987) of each client, not simply to reflect the content and feelings of what is communicated. The empathic aspect of RE in therapeutic interactions and in the skills taught to the clients is the key to its function as a method of facilitating co-constructive dialogue.

The relevance of deeply empathic responses in therapeutic and personal relationships has been the focus of attention at the Stone Center at Wellesley College for the last decade. Initially inspired by the work of Jean Baker Miller (1976), the Stone Center psychotherapists, all women, have produced a series of "Works in Progress" on the subject of empathy (Jordan, 1983; Kaplan, 1983; Miller, 1986; Surrey, 1985, 1987; Surrey, Kaplan, & Jordan, 1990). Major reviews of psychotherapy research have concluded that relational factors are the critical key to therapeutic outcome. Much work continues to be needed in applying this awareness to therapy training, clinical technique, and modalities of therapy (Kaplan, 1983) and to understanding the affective and cognitive components of the deeply empathic response.

Many reviewers and researchers on the subject of the essential aspects of effective psychotherapy have focused on the primary significance of empathy (Patterson, 1989a, 1989b; Rogers, 1961; Strupp 1986, 1989), but few theorists have paid as careful attention to the meaning of empathy as the Stone Center group. Consistent with Buber's (1965) concept of understanding the "deep inside," of another and Habermas's (1987) concept of understanding the "lifeworld," they draw attention to the affective and cognitive components of grasping the many levels and aspects of communication that are occurring when human beings interact. Not only content and feelings are being shared, but also an experience of self-in-world that is constantly in the process of changing as new experiences are integrated, new meanings constructed, and new intentions developed.

Most recently the Stone Center group has perceived the movement of mutual empathy in relationships as the ground of action and power (Surrey, Kaplan, & Jordan, 1990). They suggest replacement of the construct of "self" as it is usually conceptualized with the construct of "movement of relation." This goes beyond their original concept of "self-in-relation" to radically focus on human connectedness the core of human development and human change. This thinking is consistent with Maturana and Varela's (1987) focus on "structural coupling" as the essential factor in both biological and cultural development.

The Empathic Skill

In Relationship Enhancement couple therapy the therapist explains, demonstrates, models, and coaches the deep form of empathic interaction described above (Guerney, 1987, 1988). Following the intake interview(s), the clients are taught to empathize with each other as modeled by the therapist, to ask themselves as they listen to the other, "What would I be thinking, meaning, wanting, feeling, intending, etc. — if I were this other?" In the early weeks of skill training, empathy is applied to stories that are not related to couple conflicts but that are usually full of significance to the teller and thus are highly relevant to the couple's understanding of one another. The empathic skill alone is often revolutionary in its effect on the couple relationship. Among the effects that people report are: (a) the pleasure of having the other person understand on a level that deepens the awareness of the speaker; (b) the satisfaction and calming effect of empathizing on the empathizer. Clients often report that anger diminishes in the process of attempting to enter the subjective experience of another person; (c) a clarification of gender issues not simply on the cognitive level, but on an affect-laden experiential level as well; (d) a heightening of one's ability to think clearly as one is listened to well and listens well; (e) a diminishment of the habit of rehearsing one's response as one listens (to empathize well requires full concentration); (f) in the case of men particularly, a considerable relief that they can empathize and the awareness that perhaps all they needed was some structure and coaching; (g) in the case of women, an appreciation of the restoration of balance as they feel nurtured by the empathy of the other.

The Expressor Skill

The second skill taught that builds relationship is the "expressor skill." This has five component parts all of which contribute to the likelihood that the listener can listen non-defensively and with an interest in engaging in co-constructive dialogue.

The first element is subjectivity. Speaking as one's own point of view permits "double description." Subjectivity also increases the clients' consciousness of how meanings are co-constructed in language and in dialogue. The parable of the blind men and the elephant, in which the fight depends on the blind men forgetting (a) that they are only experiencing a piece of the reality, and (b) that they must necessarily describe that piece in language which is limited at best and always formulated out of prior experience, is useful in illustrating the concept of subjectivity. Clients are instructed in the language of subjectivity, "The way I see it, the way I remember it, from my point of view, etc." Subjectivity is of vast help in changing hierarchical patterns of relating. One can no longer speak as an infallible authority on a subject. Subjectivity is also integral to the intersubjectivity of mutual empathy. A new way of thinking emerges as one learns to speak as "one eye" in a binary system.

The second component element of the expressor guideline is the authentic ownership of feelings, and of the most vulnerable feelings one has (such as sadness, fear, and love) as well as the more defended and assertive ones (such as anger, rivalry, and aggressiveness). This is relevant to assuring that power does not get covertly acted out in the couple system. Miller (1976) focuses on the significance of overt versus covert anger in helping women assert their own needs in their lives and their relationships. Men, on the other hand, are more likely to experience covert dependency which it is useful to make overt (Dienhart and Avis, 1990).

A third element is the practice of referring to specific experiences rather than generalizing about character traits or behaviors. This specificity keeps the conversation grounded in concrete experience, and prepares the couple for the conflict resolution/ problem solving skills which require very specific thinking about what changes are wanted and how to facilitate them. Grounding one's speaking in concrete experience also permits a deeper level of empathy on the part of the listener.

The fourth element of the expressor skill is to share the "underlying positive feelings" that exist in most if not all relationships and that provide the motivational context for change. This element is useful therapeutically as well as interpersonally. It encourages the clients to touch the vulnerable "underbelly" of their feelings for one another. There is considerable cultural confusion about how one can be intimate and still autonomous, and there is a tendency in both genders to flip back and forth between unassertive dependency and assertive autonomy. The RE model effectively integrates intimacy and assertiveness in the structure of the communication skills.

The practice of asserting what one wants interpersonally is the final component of this skill. Learning to state what one wants with a focus on its interpersonal meaning and effect requires explicit consciousness of the significance of oneself, of the other person, and of the relationship. This consciousness, inherent in every aspect of the RE expressor skill, enhances the "movement of relation" described by the Stone Center theorists.

The average number of weeks that a couple participates in Relationship Enhancement couple therapy is 12 to 20. During this time the skills are applied progressively to more and more difficult topics. In addition to the primary skills of empathy and effective expression, the skills include a carefully designed format for problem solving, a structure for coaching each other at home when the skills are being practiced, and a format for supporting each other in changing habits that are experienced as dysfunctional or counter-productive. All of these skills operationalize connection-building and co-construction of new meanings.

Crisis Intervention

During the therapy, couples sometimes want to deal with a difficult issue before they have developed the skills to do so effectively. For example, Lois and Steven, the couple described above, came to their fifth session extremely upset. Steven particularly felt like the issue of their sexual relationship needed to be addressed. At these times, the RE therapist can use a crisis intervention approach (Guerney, 1977) which utilizes the skills through the process of "doubling" (Moreno, 1947) or "becoming" the client(s). In this way although the clients are likely to share their feelings in the ways with which they are most familiar (such as blaming, withdrawing, generalizing, and sharing the least rather than the most vulnerable feelings), the therapist immediately follows each such communication with an expression of the same emotions, desires, and intentions following the RE expressor guidelines. This is done in the role of the speaker speaking to the partner. A number of goals are accomplished with this technique:

1. As the therapist doubles for the client, the therapist experiences more fully the client's lifeworld.
2. The doubled client often feels as though *he* or *she* has spoken in this effective way; instead of feeling corrected by the therapist, the clients tend to feel empowered.

3. The speaker experiences the possibility of being fully authentic while at the same time monitoring his or her way of speaking so that the other person does not feel defensive.
4. The listener experiences an immediate decrease in defensiveness as the speaker's feelings and desires are doubled by the therapist.
5. The doubling process is empathic and it therefore usually has the effect of inviting the speaker to go increasingly deeper into underlying feelings.
6. New viewpoints, meanings and behaviors are co-constructed naturally in this process as they continue to be when the couple has learned to use the RE skills effectively without as much support from the therapist.

In the course of this session with Lois and Steven (the case discussed in the introduction) many feelings emerged. In the first half hour, the predominant tone on both their parts was hopelessness about the relationship. Through a combination of his own "languaging" of the problem and my doubling to his satisfaction, these are the lifeworlds that initially emerged for each of them.

Steven:

> I've given up hope about this relationship and most of the time I'm not blaming you. I just don't think you love me the way I want to be loved. And I don't think I'm asking for a lot either. When I was very sick last week, you didn't even ask me if I needed anything on Monday, yet you knew I was in this little apartment without a refrigerator or a stove. A woman from church came over with a meal and I was so touched by this little act of kindness. And I don't think you're attracted to me at all and I'm not sure you've ever been. As I think about it now I think you probably wanted to marry me because I came along at a period in your life when things were really in chaos for you and I seemed kind of stable. I think you were sexual with me because that's the way you were with everyone at that time. I don't think it had anything to do with me. I'll always be your friend and we'll continue to be parents together. I don't feel bitter; I just feel like I need to get on with my life with

someone who really loves me. I think I was hopeful initially about us getting back together because I managed to forget what was wrong the first time. I just don't feel loved beyond a kind of Platonic friendship that isn't enough for me.

Lois:

I feel really furious and also hopeless listening to you. I feel like I genuinely opened the door to us being in an intimate relationship again, and now you're slamming it shut because I haven't opened it far enough. And that's the way I've usually felt with you, like it's never enough. I can remember looking at you the day we bought our wedding rings and thinking how much I loved you and right then I thought, "I'm not good enough for him," — and that's the message I keep getting from you. You make things up in your head, — and I guess I do too. You make up that I've never loved you, that I'm not attracted to you, that I don't care about you. But you don't ask *me* what's going on with me about all that. And if I tell you, you don't believe me. I did care that you were sick and I made you a big pot of food on Sunday; Monday I was really committed to something else. I do love you, and I am attracted to you, — but I have to be with you in a way that feels honest and self-nurturing for me. When I take care of me, the message I feel like I get from you is that I've let you down.

It was useful for Steven to touch the hopelessness he felt without resisting it. He reported that he felt less hopeless just from speaking honestly about it. After doing this, he was also able to empathize well with what Lois was feeling and wanting. Once she felt understood, Lois began to be able to empathize quite successfully with Steven. Whenever the therapist or the clients feel that something important has been omitted or misunderstood in the empathizing process, the therapist either coaches changes in the empathic response, or asks the person who has spoken to clarify and amplify what it is he or she wants understood.

By the end of this session a major shift had taken place in the nature of the couple's conversation. They had become interested in the considerable differences in their perceptions, felt needs, and immediate relationship desires. They had relaxed with a process that they both realized might take some time. On the day following this session, they set several hours aside to talk. They used a spoon as a "talking stick" and carefully empathized with each other before passing the spoon to the other. Two days later, Steven again expressed the desire to make love while they were lying in bed together. Lois was infuriated by this request. For the first time, she told him, as they were lying in bed together, about her first year of becoming sexually active in college when many traumatic things had happened including a date rape. She had never told him about this for fear that he would think she had brought it on herself. After intensely expressing her anger at men, including Steven, she had begun to feel sexual again. They made love.

Steven reported in our next session that he now felt it would be all right if they didn't make love for months because he felt bonded to Lois again and that was what he had most wanted.

DISCUSSION AND CONCLUSION

The above case example was cited because it exemplifies gender-related power issues and a method for changing hierarchical relationship practices. Our long cultural history of: patriarchy, hierarchical institutions, mothers as primary parents, and various other currently prevalent practices, are myriad. They will be primary issues for couples for many decades to come. Therapeutic constructs and methods are needed to carry on and facilitate an optimally effective dialogue toward the co-construction of new meanings. Relationship Enhancement couple therapy systematically builds the skills that are necessary for such a dialogue.

Couple relationships are profoundly affected by the cultural conditioning to inhibit our authentic emotions especially when we are engaging in civilized forms of dialogue. Models of dialogic interaction are required which are respectful of the other at the same time they need to invite the full expression of feelings. Most couples need considerable practice in fully owning their own deepest emotions in their conversations with one another without shaming or blaming the other. The lack of self atunement can make it difficult to be conscious of these emotions.

It is a relatively new skill in the history of civilization, only accessible because of the development of language and thought, to have the possibility of a cognitive distance between emotions and behaviors. Since modern civilization requires the inhibition of certain behaviors, human beings have learned to inhibit their emotions as well. The practice of empathy is a powerful tool for disinhibiting emotions while preserving the essential cognitive distance between emotions and behaviors.

Furthermore mutually empathic dialogue gives a new meaning to power and empowerment. As the Stone Center theorists point out, in the context of mutually empathic dialogue "assertiveness can be reframed as empowerment in a relational context, as action to strengthen or empower the relationship rather than the separate self" (Surrey, Kaplan, & Jordan, 1990; p. 4).

Finally, the recognition of difference is integral to the forward movement of co-constructive dialogue. Gregory Bateson's construct of "multiple description" focuses on relationship as the context in which "the difference that makes a difference" is constantly emerging. A radically different experience of dialogue occurs when there is mutual empathy and the appreciation of difference. The erroneous cultural polarization of "selfish" and "unselfish," and of "me" and "you," tends to drop away and the participants become focused on the co-constructive process.

Relationship Enhancement couple therapy provides a structure and guidelines for the assertive expression of difference, the interpersonal communication of authentic emotions, and the subjective description of one's lifeworld. The dual emphasis on expression and empathy allows for the continual integration of the viewpoint of the other and the co-construction of new meanings.

REFERENCES

Allen, J. & Laird, J. (1990). Men and story: Constructing new narratives in therapy. *Journal of Feminist Family Therapy, 2*, 75-100.

Anderson, H. & Goolishian, H. (1988). Human systems as linguistic systems: Preliminary and evolving ideas about the implications for clinical theory. *Family Process, 27*, 371-394.

Anderson, H. & Goolishian, H. (1991). Thinking about multi-agency work with substance abusers and their families: A language systems approach. *Journal of Strategic and Systemic Therapies, 10,* 20-35.

Bateson, G. (1972). *Steps to an ecology of mind.* New York: Ballantine.

Bateson, G. (1979). *Mind and nature.* New York: E.P. Dutton.

Brock, G. & Joanning, H. (1983). A comparison of the Relationship Enhancement program and the Minnesota Couples Communication Program. *Journal of Marital and Family Therapy, 9,* 413-421.

Buber, M. (1965). *The knowledge of man: A philosophy of the interhuman.* New York: Harper & Row.

Chodorow, N. 1978 *The reproduction of mothering.* Berkeley, CA: University of California Press.

Dienhart, A. & Avis Myers, J. (1990). Men in therapy: Exploring feminist-informed alternatives. *Journal of Feminist Family Therapy, 2,* 25-50.

Dinnerstein, D. (1976). *The mermaid and the minotaur: Sexual arrangements and human malaise.* New York: Harper & Row.

Giblin, P., Sprenkle, D, & Sheehan, R. (1985). Enrichment outcome research: A meta-analysis of premarital, marital, and family interventions. *Journal of Marital and Family Therapy, 11,* 257-271.

Goolishian, H. & Anderson, H. (1987). Language systems and therapy: An evolving era. *Journal of Psychotherapy, 24,* 529-538.

Grunebaum, J. (1990). From discourse to dialogue: The power of fairness in therapy with couples. In R. Chasin, H. Grunebaum, & M. Herzig (Eds.), *One couple, four realities: Multiple perspectives on couple therapy* (pp. 191-228). New York: The Guilford Press.

Guerney B. G. (1977). *Relationship enhancement: Skills programs for therapy, problem prevention, and enrichment.* San Francisco: Jossey-Bass.

Guerney, B. G., Jr. (1987). Relationship enhancement: Marital/family therapist manual. State College, PA: IDEALS.

Guerney, B. G., Jr. (1988). *Relationship enhancement manual.* PA: IDEALS.

Guerney, B.G. Jr., Waldo M., & Firestone, R. (1987). Wife-battering: A theoretical construct and case report. *The American Journal of Family Therapy, 15,* 34-43.

Habermas, J. (1987). *The theory of communicative action: Volume 2, Lifeworld and system: A critique of functionalist reason* (T. McCarthy, Trans.). Boston: Beacon Press.

Hardley, G. & Guerney, B.G. Jr. (1989). A psychoeducational approach. In C.R. Figley (Ed.), *Treating stress in families* (pp. 158-181). New York: Bruner/ Mazel.

Hare-Mustin, (1987). The problem of gender in family therapy theory. In M. McGoldrick, C. Anderson, & F. Walsh (Ed.), *Women in families* (pp. 61-77). New York: W.W. Norton.

Hoffman, L. (1990). Constructing realities: An art of lenses. *Family Process, 29,* 1-12.

Jessee, R. & Guerney, B.G., Jr. (1981). A comparison of Gestalt and Relationship Enhancement treatments with married couples. *American Journal of Family Therapy, 9,* 31-41.

Jordan, J. (1983). Empathy and the mother-daughter relationship. *Work in Progress* #82-02, Wellesley, MA: Stone Center for developmental services and studies.

Kaplan, A. (1983). Empathic communication in the psychotherapy relationship. *Work in Progress* #82-02, Wellesley, MA: Stone Center for developing services and studies.

Lerner, G. (1986) *The creation of patriarchy.* New York: Oxford University Press.

Luepnitz, D. (1988). *The family interpreted: Feminist theory in clinical practice.* New York: Basic Books.

Maturana, H. & Varela, F. (1987). *The tree of knowledge: The biological roots of understanding.* Boston: New Science Library.

Miller, A. (1981). *The drama of the gifted child.* New York: Basic Books.

Miller, J. B. (1976). *Toward a new psychology of women.* Boston: Beacon Press.

Moreno, J. (1947). *The theater of spontaneity.* Beacon, New York: Beacon House.

Napier, A. (1991). Heroism, men, and marriage. *Journal of Marital and Family Therapy, 17,* 9-16.

Neal, J. & Slobodnik, A. (1990.) Reclaiming men's experience in couples therapy. *Journal of Feminist Family Therapy, 2,* 101-122.

Okin, S.M. (1989). *Justice, gender, and the family.* New York: Basic Books.

Patterson, C. (1989a). Eclecticism in psychotherapy: Is integration possible? *Psychotherapy, 26,* 157-161.

Patterson, C. (1989b). Foundations for a systematic eclectic psychotherapy. *Psychotherapy, 26,* 427-435.

Paul, J. & Paul, M. (1983). *Do I have to give up me to be loved by you?* Minneapolis: CompCare.

Rogers, C. R. (1961). *On becoming a person.* Boston: Houghton Mifflin.

Ross, E., Baker, S., & Guerney, B.G., Jr. (1985). Relationship Enhancement therapy versus therapist's preferred therapy. *American Journal of Family Therapy, 13,* 11-21.

Snyder, M. (1984). *The essential meaning(s) of the dyadic love relationship (a phenomenological study of six couples).* Unpublished doctoral dissertation. Santa Barbara, CA: Fielding Institute.

Snyder, M. (1986). Love and trust as decisions: Applications to relationship therapy. *Psychosynthesis Digest, 3,* 24-48.

Snyder, M. (1989). The Relationship Enhancement model of couple therapy: An integration of Rogers and Bateson. *Person-centered Review, 4,* 358-383.

Snyder, M. (in press-a). A gender-informed model of couple and family therapy: Relationship enhancement therapy. *Contemporary Family Therapy.*

Snyder, M. (in press-b). The relationship enhancement model of family therapy: A systematic eclectic approach. *Journal of Family Psychotherapy.*

Strupp, H. H. (1986). Psychotherapy: Research, practice, and public policy (How to avoid dead ends). *American Psychologist, 41,* 120-129.

Strupp, H. H. (1989). Psychotherapy: Can the practitioner learn from the researcher? *American Psychologist, 44,* 717-724.

Surrey, J. (1985). The "self-in-relation": A theory of women's development. *Work in Progress* #13. Wellesley, MA.: The Stone Center Working Paper Series.

Surrey, J. (1987). Relationship and empowerment. *Work in Progress* #30, Wellesley, MA.: The Stone Center Working Paper Series.

Surrey, J., Kaplan, A., & Jordan, J. (1990) *Empathy Revisited.* Wellesley, MA.: The Stone Center.

Tannen, D. (1990). *You just don't understand: Women and men in conversation.* New York: William Morrow.

Waldo, M. (1987). Also victims: Understanding and treating men arrested for spouse abuse. *Journal of Counseling and Development, 65,* 385-388.

White, M. (1986). Negative explanation, restraint and double description: A template for family therapy. *Family Process, 25,* 169-184.

The Rise of the Conscious Feminine

Sharon Conarton

SUMMARY. The rise of the conscious feminine in the world is welcome and overdue. However, the change in the balance of power between men and women in relationship is presenting the need to develop a better understanding of the archetypal characteristics of the masculine and feminine as well as the differences between men and women. This article explores some of the developmental differences, the maintenance of mutuality and learning connecting skills.

Sixteen or so years ago when I first studied Jungian psychology, I attended a seminar on alchemy. The professor commented, "The feminine doesn't think." My unbelieving angry response of "What do you mean the feminine doesn't think?" was the beginning of my focusing on the masculine and feminine archetypes. A few years before I had presented a paper for a panel at an Orthopsychiatry conference. The main thesis was that there were very few differences between men and women with the exception of men having a ten percent higher basal metabolism rate, more muscle mass and, of course, genital differences. There were also some hormonal studies being done at that time—which may or may not have evidenced innate behavioral mechanisms. I was very much into the "equality" of men and women. Somehow equality was being equated as "the same."

Another event happened at about the same time. I was driving

Sharon Conarton, BSN, LCSW, is a social worker with a private practice in Jungian psychotherapy in Denver, CO. In her 20 years of experience as a clinical social worker and 14 years as a nurse, she has been involved in direct clinical care, teaching, supervision and consultation. She is also Director of The Center for Relational Therapy and Research in Denver which provides gender appropriate therapy and education in gender studies.

down the mountains to my office in the city when a phrase came to me: "Feminism is not the struggle for equality between men and women; it is the teleological movement toward the whole."

It is the "movement toward the whole" that I am addressing in this paper. Every living organism has an innate drive to be whole. I see the tremendous changes in relationships, marriage and individual development to be related to this transformation.

Understanding the phenomena of wholeness in relationship or an individual necessitates identifying the parts of the whole. In a traditional heterosexual relationship the parts are men and women. Individually the archetypes of the masculine and feminine are the particular parts of the whole. Jungian psychology speaks of the archetype as an unconscious idea pattern of thought or image which is instinctual and universally present in individual psyches (Jung, 1954). Jung asserted that all the essential psychic characteristics that distinguish us as human beings are determined by genetics and are with us from birth. Personal experience develops what is already there, actualizing the archetypal potential already present in the person in a manner similar to that by which a photographer, through the addition of chemicals and use of skill, brings out the image impregnated in a photographic plate.

The masculine and feminine archetypes or principles are mutually complementary, homeostatically balanced and mutually interdependent. One is not superior to the other. Sigmund Freud (1925) presented a similar idea in his belief that human beings, because of their bisexual constitution and crossed inheritance, unite male and female characteristics. This view also coincides with the ancient Chinese Taoist concepts of yin and yang, those fundamental feminine and masculine principles which are held to permeate all reality and to be present and active in both men and women (Stevens, 1982).

The following is an outline of masculine and feminine archetypal characteristics (Table 1).

When the masculine and feminine archetypes are not integrated or balanced in an individual or society, a malfunction results. In our culture it is Patriarchy — a condition where feminine values are denied, denigrated and repressed. The result is malignant overgrowth of the masculine. We must be cautious not to throw the "baby out

TABLE I

PATRIARCHAL	MASCULINE	FEMININE
Denial of Feminine	Light Sun	Dark Moon
1. External Focus	External	Internal
2. Narcissism	Autonomy	Relationship
3. Rational Objectivity	Thinking	Feeling
4. Ego Centered	Ego	Selfless
5. "Me" Generation	Self Oriented	Other Oriented
6. Closed	Boundaries	Merging
7. Win At All Costs	Competition	Cooperation
8. Status Oriented	Hierarchal	Circular
9. End Justifies Means	Goal Oriented	Process Oriented
10. Planned Obsolescence	Production	Nature/Natural
11. Ecological Disaster	Unlimited World Resource	Limited World Resource
12. Projection of Shadow	Perfection	Wholeness
13. Mind/Body Split	Mind	Body
14. Scientific Proof	Intellectual Knowledge	Intuitive Knowing
15. Bureaucracy	Order	Chaos
16. Rigidity	Control	Spontaneity
17. Rules	Structure	Fluidity
18. Fear of Change	Status Quo	Dynamic Changing
19. Military Mentality	Domination	Submission
20. Right by Might	Aggressive	Passive
21. Striving for Power	Power Over	Power For
22. War	Killing	Rage
23. Loss of Human Value	Denial of Death	Death

(Sharon A. Conarton Work in Progress - critiques encouraged) with the bath water" when we strive for a "non-Patriarchal" society. Patriarchy does not mean masculine; it is the dishonoring and devaluing of the feminine. The positive aspects of the masculine need to be preserved and integrated with the rising feminine consciousness.

Riane Eisler (1987), in her highly successful book, *The Chalice and the Blade*, traces the unseen forces that shape human culture from prehistory through recorded history and into the future. She speaks of basically three epochs. The first, a 20,000 year partnership society where men and women related in an egalitarian though unconscious instinctual world. Then the past "bloody 5,000-year detour" of male and masculine domination, and now an emerging consciousness whereby we are reclaiming lost feminine values. She does not see this as a developing matriarchy in contrast to the patriarchy but as a true conscious partnership society.

This change in the culture and the individual is bringing about changes in relationship. As clinical therapists it is necessary for us to know the differences between the masculine and the feminine, and between men and women in order to teach our clients about the tremendous transformation taking place both in the culture and interpersonally.

The ideal relationship of the past assumed men would play out the "male role" and women would play out the "female role." The feminine was assigned to women, the masculine to men. Women who developed their masculine and focused on cognitive, rational, productive aspects of their personality were seen as inferior women, somehow lacking in nurturing and feeling abilities. Men who were sensitive, compassionate and caring were viewed as wimps and sissies.

In the fifties women, ideally, were getting the same education as men but there was always the unstated directive that a mother should prepare her daughter for a patriarchal market: she would get married, have a family and play out her expected role. She would have her education to fall back on if anything happened to her husband. Well, it didn't happen to her husband — it happened to her.

The women's movement, based on democracy and equality between men and women as well as the rise of the feminine consciousness, began to affect women. As women went back to work, school, and out into the service community, they developed a sense of their own identities in the world. They also influenced their daughters. In the sixties if a woman chose to take on the traditionally male task of working in the market place, she was still expected to carry out the traditional roles of the caretaker and emotional supporter of the family. Her daughter could see that this was not only inequitable, it was impossible. Today's young wife and mother is searching for a more equitable relationship.

It has been women, of course, who down through the ages fought for their liberation and equality. Briffault (1956) wrote in 1930 about criticism of marriage coming "from the women of England. It is called forth by certain features of our marriage institutions which, while they make husband and wife one, seem to provide that the husband shall be that one." Our contemporary conscious woman is not asking just for liberation and equality, she is asking her partner to partake in liberation and equality also. She does not want a dominant/submissive type of partnership. She is asking for mutuality and equal responsibility of both partners for the maintenance of the relationship.

Theoretically, everyone would agree that a relationship should be based on mutuality, commitment and equality. In actuality that does not happen. We continue to hear in couples therapy of the woman saying, "I want more," and the man saying, "I've given you everything, how can I give you any 'more'?" He would give it to her if he could. My ten years of facilitating men's groups has assured me of that. He doesn't know what she's talking about. Men continually tell me they want the same thing women want—a close, loving relationship, sharing the financial, emotional and caretaking aspects, a future together. So, what's wrong?

Women have taken care of the emotional needs of men for as long as we know. Men have appeared to be independent, autonomous and standing on their own two feet—but there has always been a woman there taking care of them: mother, sister, wife, daughter, girlfriend, secretary, flight attendant, etc. They may have been vocationally and financially independent but the fact is they have remained emotionally and relationship dependent and, in many ways, have very little concept of the skills required to mutually relate to another on an emotional feeling level. Women no longer want the total responsibility for the maintenance and growth of the relationship.

If the old ways do not work and we have no role models we are going to have to develop a theory of relationship and start teaching people the skills needed. In the same way that women have had to look to men to see how to operate in a patriarchal market place, men are going to have to learn from women the art and skill of relating and connecting.

The first determination we must make, a point we therapists often take for granted, is: does this couple want to be in relationship? Unlike their forebearers, women are learning that an unsatisfactory relationship is not better than being alone.

Elisabeth Badinter (1989), in *The Unopposite Sex*, champions single life:

> The spectre of solitude has given way to the hell of a failed life as a couple. The end of symbiosis, marked by the absence of dialogue, plunges us into a kind of solitude that is far more unbearable than if we were really living alone, freed from the constraints imposed by the presence of the Other. It is no longer the harshness of solitary life that we contrast with the pleasure of a harmonious, fused life, it is the distress caused by the failure of a loving relationship. This is what we now see as real coldness, by comparison with which solitude seems almost warm. . . . And anyway, what is the good of trying to patch things up temporarily when their hearts are no longer on the same wave length? An unstable couple has lost its reason for remaining a couple. To pretend to ignore this smacks of a hypocrisy counter to our cult of authenticity. (p. 211)

Of course, not everyone feels that way. Many couples are willing to sacrifice some of their individual goals of achievement and authenticity for a growing mutual relationship, particularly if they have children. The vision of creating a family atmosphere which is non-patriarchal, spiritual and nurturing for *all* members is becoming the ideal goal for many couples.

A relationship is an actual entity with life sustaining requirements: it doesn't just happen. Each person must be actively involved in creating mutuality. We can no longer just simply play out roles assigned to us by gender.

An exciting exploration of relationship theory is coming from the Stone Center in Wellesley, MA. In *What Do We Mean By Relationships?*, Jean Baker Miller (1986) describes the characteristics of growth-fostering relationships. "It proposes that relationships lead to an increase in 'zest' (or vitality), empowerment, knowledge, worth and sense of connection with others. An examination of the interactions in growth-fostering relationships suggests that the essential feature is the interplay of mutual empathy created by both (or all) participants."

Miller speaks of "empowerment," as we are hearing so frequently these past few years. Traditionally, the masculine sense of power refers to domination, control, or mastery implying "power over." The feminine sense of power is to "empower the other." We see examples of the use of both aspects of power being used by the successful corporate executive who uses his power over other people to bring about a sense of community and loyalty within the group as well as empowering his employees to be individually successful. He integrates his masculine sense of power with his feminine values. In the past women have been depended upon to help their mate to success or promote the self actualization of their children or employers, etc. They have not wanted to compete for themselves or stand out above others for fear of losing their connections. In the past two decades many patriarchal women have learned to emulate this masculine power for domination and control and as a result often abandon their feminine to become pseudo men (Conarton & Silverman, 1988). In order to have a growth oriented relationship we must be involved in mutual empowerment, each *for* the other. Ideally, that would mean a sense of personal power and a desire to empower the other.

If we determine the couple does want to be in relationship we need to help them learn some relationship theory, concepts and skills. In my experience, I find three basic elements necessary:

I. Knowledge of differences between men and women;
II. The maintenance of mutuality in spite of differences;
III. Learning connecting skills.

I. DIFFERENCES BETWEEN MEN AND WOMEN

In order to reclaim feminine values it is necessary to teach our clients the archetypal characteristics of both the masculine and feminine — not just men, but also women. In recent years many women adopted masculine values and became male identified and strived for the same prizes as men in the patriarchy. They repressed and abandoned their feminine side much as men have. Men, in striving to be more connected, have adapted the feminine in a manner that has resulted in them being what Robert Bly (1990) calls "soft men."

Masculine characteristics are most common to men, the feminine to women. Jungians refer to each person's secondary characteristics as the contra sexual. Ideally, when women develop their contra sexual characteristics they manifest them differently than we see the masculine traits in men manifested, and when they develop their contra sexual characteristics it doesn't look the same as it does in women.

It would seem from Table I that men are most comfortable when autonomous, when they are separate and have firm boundaries, whereas women most desire close intimate relationships. The most definitive difference in masculine and feminine traits is the concept of "self and other." The feminine is "other oriented." This characteristic combined with the tendency to merge and not maintain boundaries manifests in women becoming very much more aware of the needs of the other, and is there for the other person before her own self, being able to perceive the other's feelings before her own, wanting to maintain a continuous feeling connection. The masculine is "self oriented" characterized as a firm sense of boundaries and an awareness of needs that manifests in men as Ego — knowing what they want and how to get it. This sense of order and control, along with goal orientation, facilitates the ability to focus.

Teaching the concept of the masculine and feminine archetypal traits is tricky business. It's even hard for us to keep in mind that feminine does not mean female and masculine does not mean male. Most people feel complimented by masculine traits, particularly men, and feel demeaned when associated with feminine traits. However, as the consciousness changes, masculine/feminine is more generally accepted: we see males appreciating their "nurturing" and "intuitive" abilities (feminine traits) as well as females striving to develop their "focusing" and "goal oriented" abilities (masculine traits).

"As in physical, spiritual and emotional development, relationship, too, has a hierarchy of levels, understanding and being" (Zaleski, 1988). Evolution of self is a difficult process. The evolution of two selves in relationship can be quite perilous as two people embark on an exploration from one level to the next. And the two individuals may not be at the same level at the same time.

Early in the relationship women, as they fall in love, exemplify the unconscious instinctual characteristics of the feminine. They are other oriented, fascinated with the other, caretaking, selfless to the point of not knowing who they are anymore, submissive, in denial, and literally out of their minds. It's a wonderful state for young lovers, wives and mothers to be in. During courtship men evidence abilities to be there for the other, to be mutually engaged and concerned with the direction and growth of the relationship, but after marriage or the solidifying of the relationship, they seem to slip back into a narcissistic self orientation that lasts at least until their thirties or to a midlife crisis. Many women remember these years as the happiest of their life. As the relationship matures, if the woman has integrated a sense of the masculine, she will begin to pull back her boundaries and have more awareness of her own self and what she wants. She will also be reclaiming her projections and utilizing less denial.

She will start saying, "I want to be me" — much to her partner's surprise. He hasn't realized that she has been so "other oriented," that she did not have much awareness of her own needs and wants. Now she wants the relationship to change. Understandably this is a very disturbing situation for the man and the woman. The prototype for the traditional patriarchal relationship is of the woman providing maternal nurturing — a mommy wife, so to speak. When she begins to develop a conscious sense of her self she becomes less oriented to the needs of her partner and more to the need for movement and growth in the relationship. Most men, being more influenced by the masculine status quo, see no need for the relationship to change. As the woman changes, the man she is with experiences her pulling away. He is bewildered by her being there for herself when he needs her. She has always been there for him first. The pain he feels is severe. He doesn't see that he is there for himself and she is there for herself; he experiences that something has been taken away from him — like his heart ripped out. When he feels she hurt him he'll want to "fight back" or get even (most likely by withdrawing, withholding and being passive aggressive).

The woman feels lonely, alienated and abandoned. She does not enjoy him being there for himself and her being there for herself. Without a connection, for her, there is nothing in the relationship. Her partner feels unappreciated for what he does provide for her. She is yearning for him to connect with her. Since he most likely does not know what she is talking about, he can't do it. She, of course, thinks this is purposive and intentional. She becomes enraged. The power struggle begins.

II. MAINTAINING MUTUALITY IN SPITE OF DIFFERENCES

At this stage of the relationship we do not see the couple mutually connected or empathic with the other. There is too much anger and fear in both the man and the woman. As they sit with us in the consulting room we can most readily experience the woman's anger at being disconnected, not seen and not responded to, and the man's fear and sense of being overwhelmed and unappreciated. In order to facilitate some sense of compassion of one for the other we must help them understand their conceptual and gender differences in reference to connection, separation, power, intimacy, sexuality, change, competition, boundaries, etc.

Neither knows how powerful the other sees them as. Men who are not abusive usually are not aware that women are inhibited and frightened by their physical power. That is one of the reasons women have learned to be submissive. Men may deny it is a threat or that it even exists, or they may have learned in boyhood to fear their own physical power. On the other hand, women would be quite surprised to "hear men talk of women with dread and horror and awe, as if women were powerful as the sea and inescapable as fate" (Lederer, 1968).

Men see power as power over. They may well mistake women's attempts to control their own life, to maintain a sense of sovereignty, as an attempt to have power over them. In the fairy tale *Hags and Heroes*, Sir Gwain is given a choice: His bride (his feminine) may be a hag by day and a lovely maiden by night, or a beautiful accommodating wife for all to see by day and an ugly hideous hag by night. The wise Sir Gwain gives *her* the choice since it's her life. He is rewarded with a temperate spontaneous loving wife by both night and day. Modern men might be surprised how they would be rewarded if they heeded Sir Gwain's example and gave their feminine full reign (Young-Eisendrath, 1984).

A very crucial difference exists between the masculine and feminine and, as a result, between men and women in their sense of separation and connection. Object relations theory, based on male norms, stresses separation and individuation as primary goals of children's identity formation (Mahler, 1975). However, Chodorow (1978), in *The Reproduction of Mothering*, maintains that while separation and individuation are fundamental goals in the psychological development of all individuals, there are marked differences in maternal relationships with sons and daughters.

Since then other feminist writers have recognized the differences in mother/daughter relationship and the role this plays in the individuation process of men and women (Eichenbaum & Orbach, 1983; Kaplan & Surrey, 1984; Rubin, 1983). Males appear to begin the separation process in early infancy, but females usually do not begin the major part of this process until midlife (Chodorow, 1978).

Differences in the separation processes of boys and girls appear to account for some of the differences in the behavior of adult males and females.

> A boy child is different from a girl child. He is "the other," and from early on, the mother knows that he is the other. The girl child is not perceived as "the other"; she is perceived as being the same as the mother. Manifesting more of the archetypal feminine characteristics than the boy, the girl is more certainly identified with the mother; both mother and daughter operate with more open emotional connection and boundary flexibility. The sense of being the same as mother necessitates

her taking on the feelings of mother. If mother is angry, she is angry; if mother is guilty, she is guilty. Without the basic preliminary separation, the intrapsychic bond between mother and daughter becomes stronger and stronger. (Conarton & Silverman, 1988, p.45)

This emotional sensitivity develops into cognitive and affective interactions that we later identify as empathy. The connectedness and the capacity for identification is the basis for the later feeling that to understand and to be understood are crucial for self acceptance and are fundamental to the feeling of existing as a part of a unit or a network larger than the individual (Kaplan & Surrey, 1984).

The developmental cycle of women must be viewed with the awareness that women experience their sense of self in relationship. "The basic feminine sense of self is connected to the world; the basic masculine sense of self is separate" (Chodorow, 1978).

That is to say: the masculine aspect of the self must be there for the self in order to have adequate ego strength, to have a sense of being an individual. This is a comfortable state for men. The feminine aspect of self must be available to connect with the other in order to experience a mutual relationship, an experience most natural for women. Each must learn to develop the contra sexual. For a woman to develop this masculine sense of self she must "pull back boundaries," so to speak, and pay attention to being there for her own self. Women do not like to hear this. They feel their perceptive, intuitive, connecting abilities to be their most valued skill in relating and feel they are being asked to not be who they are. They also feel selfish and guilty. Those around them reinforce these feelings. Men often feel this type of connecting to be intrusive and overwhelming. Only when a woman pulls back this energy can the man learn to risk extending his feeling self out to meet a woman in a mutually empathic relationship. Many men never experience a need to connect because the women in their lives are already connecting with them to the extent they feel no loss. Only when men feel the pain of not having a feeling connection can they understand what it is women are talking about when they speak of a "mutually empathic relationship."

In order to maintain this empathic mutuality as a couple they must have an empathic attitude toward their own growing and changing selves. Moving out of the stereotyped roles of traditional relationship is contrary to collective patriarchal norms. Women, since they are more in touch with their feminine energy, are more prone to change — much to the confusion of their partner. They may take a totally different stand one month to the next, or discover a new aspect of their self. They may not like what they see and how they feel and will need help to develop some compassion and acceptance of their emerging sense of self with its negative as well as positive feelings. Men, as they allow themselves to experience long repressed feelings, need tremendous support to understand they are not weak, crazy or falling into an abyss. Only when they have empathy toward their own humanness can they have empathy and tolerance for the struggle of the other and develop a mutual sense of relationship. Judith Jordan (1986) defines mutuality as,

> a mutual exchange where one is both affecting the other and being affected by the other; one extends oneself out to the other and is also receptive to the impact of the other. There is openness to influence, emotional availability and a constantly changing pattern of responding to and affecting the other's state. There is both receptivity and active initiative toward the other. (p. 1)

Each responds and *each* extends their self out to the other.

There has to be some compassion for the anguish and disappointment of the other as women and men see that the other is not who they thought they were. In Jungian terms, women project their animus (undeveloped masculine) on men and men project their anima (undeveloped feminine) onto women. Added to this is a necessary level of denial which aids the mechanism of attraction. As the relationship grows more intimate, matures and projections are reclaimed, they each begin to see the other with a new awareness of reality. "The American dream has turned into the American nightmare," in the words of a client as he and his wife reached beyond the stage of living "happily ever after." In order to have compassion and see what men *can* give them, women must resolve some of the anger and disappointment they feel when they discover men not to be who they thought they were. In the process, as they realize men cannot give them what they were looking for—that they must actually be able to take the necessary steps to do this for themselves—they begin to have more belief in their own self and their own abilities. In the process of looking at these differences, particularly between his own sexual needs and those of his wife's, another client was astounded that a man has to make love to a woman's mind. At this point his wife could have some compassion when he went about it in an orderly, methodical, goal oriented, masculine manner by writing out a schedule for romance—starting with a compliment in the morning, flowers during the day, asking about her feelings at dinner, and remembering to make an appropriate response to her.

I find that clients become really excited as the differences unfold, particularly if they can maintain their sense of humor. Men seem to be more aware that women are different from them. It may be that because women can often sense men's feelings—even when the man is unaware of them—that women misinterpret how different men are from them. Often they expect men's feeling responses to be like women's and are quite surprised and disappointed when they are not. The feminine is manifested differently in men.

I have a Sylvia card by the cartoonist Nicole Hollander which shows Sylvia as a gypsy with a crystal ball. A young woman is asking her when men will talk about their feelings. Sylvia answers, "Next year at 2:00 p.m. men will start talking about their feelings." On the inside of the card Sylvia says, "And at 2:05 women all over America will be sorry."

It's not an easy task for men or women. These diversities are a source of creative energy, as well as conflict, for the relationship and a means to teaching connecting skills in therapy.

III. LEARNING CONNECTING SKILLS

In addition to our usual repertoire of strategies and techniques for couples therapy, we need to bring the client's attention to the energy exchange as they feel the connection going on between them. It may seem elementary to us as clinical therapists but for most people it isn't. At a recent seminar for professional advancement, "New Visions of the Male-Female Relationship: Creating Mutuality" (Bergman & Surrey, 1990), in a written exercise, the most frequently listed question from men (after "Why are women so angry?") was, "What do women mean by 'connecting'?" Generally, men know what sexual connection means but do not know what emotional connection means.

I would again like to use the Stone Center because they describe the process so well. Surrey (1984) directs attention to how people learn this ability to connect. She delineates the key processes in psychological development when seen as "development within relationship which is where all psychological development occurs." The key elements are: the development of empathic abilities, the developmental process of mutual empathy, and the resultant emergence of mutual empowerment and self-knowledge. Surrey describes mutual empathy as follows: "'Being with' means 'being seen' and 'feeling seen' (which women claim they don't feel) by the other and 'seeing the other' and sensing the other 'feeling seen'" (p.4). The exact situation is difficult to describe. We know it when we see it and can point it out to each couple as they interact. Particularly we need to name these interactions as men and women experience them. We need to name each step of the process: "This is empathy," "This is the experience of feeling mutual empathy," "This is what 'being connected' feels like." We can use our self as we interact with the individual client or each of them as they relate to each other. Using couples groups is an even more efficient mechanism for teaching men what it looks like to bring response-ability to the relationship, and to demonstrate to women that it's not just her partner who becomes overwhelmed with dread. Couples groups give an opportunity to observe what it means to hold onto the relational moment to improve the quality of the connection. They see the result of interaction in other couples. They see the mirroring of some of their own attitudes and blocks. The bonding of the women enables each individual woman to speak up and say how she feels in a way she would never attempt without other women's presence and support, particularly if she has been in a women's group. The men being together often utilizes their competitiveness for creative risk taking. The presence of other men who also understand the fear of women alleviates some of the men's fears of "being found out." A group can precipitate material for couple therapy that would never come up without the exposure to the other couples. And because some of this material is new to many people there is not as much resistance in groups.

When a man integrates his feminine energy with his predominantly masculine self he relates with a very powerful penetrating emotional energy which is frightening to women not familiar with this kind of energy transaction. The situation brings up a whole new creative direction to the relationship. It precipitates anxiety in women who are not used to receiving or experiencing men who are knowledgeable about connecting. As women learn to have voluntary control over their giving feminine energies, men will have to learn to recognize what it is they want from women and be able to ask for it. Women, then, can choose what they are willing to give and to whom. Hopefully feminine energies will be more valued and reclaimed by both men and women. We can see that the resolution of conflict in one level of the relationship opens the couple up to the possibilities of a new level of intimacy and, of course, more differences. Not all couples have the desire, time or environmental opportunity to individuate and maintain this ideal of personal growth together.

We, as therapists, have the responsibility and the wonderful good fortune to be part of the transformation that is evolving. We need the courage to stand up for feminine values when most of the patriarchy is still denying and denigrating the necessity for this radical change in tradition. Accepting the conscious feminine for ourselves is the first step in the healing process of our clients.

REFERENCES

Badinter, E. (1989). *The Unopposite sex: The end of the gender battle*. New York: Harper & Row.

Belenky, M.F., Clinchy, B.M., Goldberger, N.R., & Tarule, J.M. (1986). *Women's ways of knowing*. New York: Basic Books.

Bergman, S.J., & Surrey, J.L. (1990). *New visions of the male-female relationship: Creating mutuality*. Seminar held August 17,18,19 in Wellfleet, MA.

Bly, Robert. (1990). *Iron John*. Reading: Addison-Wesley.

Briffault, R., & Malinowski, B. (1956). *Marriage: Past and present: A debate between Robert Briffault and Bronislaw Malinowski*. Boston: Porter Sargent.

Chodorow, N. (1978). *The Reproduction of mothering: Psychoanalysis and the sociology of gender*. Berkeley, CA: University of California Press.

Conarton, S., & Silverman, L.K. (1988). Feminine development through the life cycle. In: *Feminist psychotherapies: Integration of therapeutic and feminist systems* (pp. 37-67), M.A. Dutton-Douglas & L.E.A. Walker, Eds. Norwood, NJ: Ablex Publishing Corp.

Eichenbaum, L., & Orbach, S. (1983). *What do women want: Exploding the myth of dependency*. New York: Berkley Books.

Eisler, Riane. (1987). *The Chalice and the blade: Our history, our future*. New York: Harper & Row.

Freud, S. (1925). Three contributions to the sexual theory. *Nervous and Mental Disease Monograph Series*, No. 7. New York: Nervous & Mental Disease Publishing Co.

Jordan, J.V. (1986). The meaning of mutuality. *Work in Progress*, No. 23. Wellesley, MA: Stone Center Working Papers Series.

Jung, C.G. (1954). Marriage as a psychological relationship. *The development of personality. The collected works of C.G. Jung* (Vol. 17). (R.F.C. Hull, trans.). New York: Bollingen Foundation.

Kaplan, A.G., & Surrey, J.L. (1984). The relational self in women: Developmental theory and public policy. In: *Women and mental health policy* (pp. 79-94), L.E. Walker, Ed. Beverly Hills, CA: Sage.

Lederer, W. (1968). *The Fear of women*. New York: Harcourt Brace Jovanovich.

Mahler, M.S., Pine, F., & Bergman, A. (1975). *The Psychological birth of the human infant: Symbiosis and individuation*. New York: Basic Books.

Miller, J. B. (1986). What do we mean by relationships?. *Work in Progress*, No. 22. Wellesley, MA: Stone Center Working Papers Series.

Rubin, L. (1983). *Intimate strangers: Men and women together*. New York: Harper & Row.

Stevens, A. (1982). *Archetypes: A natural history of the self*. New York: Morrow.

Surrey, J.L. (1984). Self-in-relation: A theory of women's development. *Work in Progress*, No. 13. Wellesley, MA: Stone Center Working Papers Series.

Young-Eisendrath, P. (1984). *Hags and heroes: A feminist approach to Jungian psychotherapy with couples*. Toronto: Inner City Books.

Zaleski, P. (1988). Easy answers. *Parabola: Myth and the Quest for Meaning, 13* (3), 84-91.

Couples Relationships of AFDC Mothers

Geoffrey L. Greif
Susan Zuravin

SUMMARY. Virtually nothing is known about AFDC mothers and their relationships with their male friends. Yet such men are clearly an influence in their lives. Findings from a sample of 275 Baltimore AFDC mothers provide important exploratory data about the characteristics of these relationships and about how women who have a long-term male friend differ from AFDC mothers who do not. Implications for work with these couples are also presented.

Despite the vast amount of literature being amassed on working with couples, virtually nothing empirical has been published on very low-income heterosexual couples. This paper addresses this gap in the literature by describing the nonmarital relationships of mothers receiving Aid to Families with Dependent Children (AFDC) and by comparing these mothers' experiences with other AFDC mothers who are not involved in long-term relationships. This couple's relationship will be framed from the perspective of the mother.

With nearly half of the nation's single parent families living in poverty (Bane and Ellwood, 1989) these mothers and the significant men in their life are a critical population to study. More common than a husband, a male friend (defined here as a male lover or boyfriend of at least three months duration), plays a valuable and un-

Geoffrey L. Greif, DSW, and Susan Zuravin, PhD, are affiliated with the University of Maryland at Baltimore, School of Social Work, 525 W. Redwood St., Baltimore, MD 21201.

The authors would like to thank Edward Pawlak for his helpful suggestions on an earlier version of this article.

Address correspondence to Geoffrey L. Greif.

studied role in the everyday lives of these women. Marital relationships are not the norm. For example, according to a 1980 random sample of Wisconsin welfare recipients, only a small percentage, 13%, of these heads of households who either had or were expecting children, were expected to marry within a given three year period (Rank, 1987). Data from the same study show that female-headed households on welfare are more prevalent than married-ones by a 2 to 1 ratio (Rank, 1986). It is not only that many never marry. Among those that do, some argue that the welfare system heightens their chances of getting divorced (Bahr, 1979). While this linear relationship has been disputed (Draper, 1981), it is irrefutable that the nonmarital relationship that develops between the AFDC mother and her male friend is one that needs to be better understood.

A primary relationship, one that develops between a couple, can serve as a source of support and nurturance that can sustain the members through good and bad times. Poverty is a constant, unrelenting stress. The need for poor people to have a reliable partner is especially acute. Yet welfare policies in many states make it more difficult for mothers to receive AFDC if there is a man in the house. As a result, mothers often hide their relationships with boyfriends. The "Man in the House" rule turns these adult relationships into shadowy ones where descriptions of the man arise only when child protective services is involved or questions around AFDC eligibility are raised.

Mental health practitioners working with the mother alone or with these couples are faced with many stereotypes that need clarifying. First, it is often believed that women on AFDC are involved in chaotic relationships. Second, it is thought that they lead promiscuous lives within these relationships. Third, violence is thought to be a common element with the mother the victim. These stereotypes can have an impact on the practitioner's counter-transference, on how the couple is approached, and on the types of interventions that are considered. Thus the need to know about these couples is great as not only are practitioners often working in the dark, they may be operating under invalid assumptions.

A review of the relevant literature turned up little information on this facet of the population. We searched for information first on AFDC mothers and then on low-income males in nonmarital relationships. A few studies have focused on the child maltreating AFDC mother in an attempt to understand the relationship between the male friend and the part he plays in the maltreatment cycle. Less information exists on AFDC mothers who do not maltreat, a normative group. What is known about them often comes from panel studies or demographic descriptions of welfare recipients where their relationships with men are not described. While data does exist on the teenage father (see, for example, Robinson, 1988), virtually nothing was found on the adult male friend involved with these AFDC mothers. The one exception was Zuravin and Greif (1989) who compared the level of violence in normative AFDC mothers' relationships with their boyfriends with the level in the relationships of mothers who were known to child protective services for maltreatment. A higher degree of verbal violence between normal mothers and their boyfriends was found than between maltreating mothers and theirs. All other forms of violence were more frequent in the maltreating mothers' relationships than in the nonmaltreating mothers.

As a great deal of the research on single parents has been based on middle-class samples (e.g., Wallerstein and Kelly, 1980), mental health practitioners treating couples are left with broad brush descriptions that are not specific about the interpersonal dynamics of the low-income couple's relationship. Practitioners, lacking other ideas, would naturally tend to consider applying these interventions to the AFDC mother. To begin to correct this situation or to deal with stereotypes that may be inaccurate, answers for two questions are sought here:

1. What is the nature of the couple relationship between the AFDC and her long-term male friend?
2. What are the differences, if any, between AFDC mothers with male friends and those without them?

METHODOLOGY

Information for this exploratory study comes from a fairly extensive set of interview data (Zuravin & Taylor, 1987) gathered during 1984 and 1985. The sample consisted of two groups: 237 mothers who were known to public child protective services for having one or more physically abused and/or neglected children and 281 mothers none of whom had ever had involvement with any public child welfare service. Analyses for this report were carried out on the group of 281 subjects. Six of this group were married so the final sample was 275. The 237 maltreating respondents were excluded because comparisons of maltreating and nonmaltreating AFDC mothers (Wolock & Horowitz, 1977; Zuravin & Greif, 1989) as well as other low-income women (Kotelchuck, 1982; Starr, 1982) suggest that the two groups differ with respect to a wide variety of psychosocial and interpersonal characteristics that could affect not only their dating patterns but also the characteristics of their heterosexual relationships. We also wanted to study a more normative population, one whose relationships were not affected by the sequelae of child maltreatment.

The 275 subjects of this report were self-selected from a sample of 376 female Aid to Families of Dependent Children (AFDC) recipients (74.7% interview completion rate). This sample was screened into the study from a 2.1% systematic sample (selection of every 46th family beginning with a random start) of the 37,158 female-headed families who were receiving AFDC but not child protective services during January 1984 in Baltimore, Maryland. None of the families had ever been a recipient (either in the past or during the sampling month) of any of the child welfare services (including foster care, child protection, single parent services as well as services to families with children) provided by the Baltimore City Department of Social Services. Even though efforts were made to select a sample of respondents who would be representative of the typical AFDC recipient, the cross-sectional nature of our study has probably resulted in over-representation of the longer term recipient.

Measures

Dating patterns. The primary objective of the dating questionnaire items was to gain information on the prevalence of nonmarital, heterosexual, intimate relationships among the population of female head-of-the-household AFDC recipients. As noted earlier, this type of relationship is of particular interest because of the low marriage rate for this group of women. The main screening question, from the National Probability Survey of Unmarried Young Women (Tanfer, 1983) was asked of all women who did not classify themselves as married at the time they were interviewed. It read: Are you currently involved in a relationship with a man that has lasted three months or longer during which you have had intercourse at least once? The three month or longer duration criterion was imposed to exclude episodic encounters and short-term relationships (Tanfer, 1987). To obtain dating information on the women who said they were not involved in a relationship at the time of the interview, those who answered "no" to the above screening question, we asked:

(Aside from your marriage), have you ever had a relationship with a man that lasted for three months or longer during which you had intercourse at least one time?

To determine whether these women were currently dating, they were asked, "are you currently going out or dating?" The five response options were almost every day, once or twice per week, once or twice per month, less than once per month, and not at all.

Personal characteristics. Following Tanfer (1987), women were asked a series of questions that focused on eliciting information about demographic, psychosocial, and fertility-related characteristics. Four psychosocial characteristics were examined—self-esteem, psychological distress, the existence and characteristics of confidante relationships, and degree of respondent's desire to change her relationship with men. The first three were included to obtain some insight into the effect of an intimate, heterosexual relationship on the low-income woman's feelings of well-being and mastery. At least some of the literature on low-income women (e.g., Brown & Harris, 1978) suggests that such a relationship has a positive effect. Confidante relationships were explored not only because the literature suggests that they have a beneficial effect on well-being (e.g., Brown & Harris, 1978) but also to determine if the male friend plays the role of confidante. Respondent's desire to change her relationship with men was included so that we could test the hypothesis that women who were having no relationship were more likely to identify the need to change their relationship with men.

Self-esteem was measured with an index compiled from responses to five items from the Rosenberg Self-Esteem scale (Rosenberg, 1979). Subjects responded to the items on a five point scale ranging from strongly disagree to strongly agree. The index was constructed by summing scores. Higher scores (scores can range from 0 to 25) indicate a higher degree of self-liking and self-acceptance. Degree of psychological distress was measured with the Beck Depression Inventory (BDI)(Beck, 1970), a frequently used 21 item measure of severity of depressive symptoms on the day of the interview. BDI scores are constructed by adding response scores (range from 0 to 3) for the 21 items. Scores of 14 or greater are considered to be clinically significant. The existence and nature of confidante relationships was examined with a series of questions from the Diagnostic Interview Schedule (DIS)(1981). The DIS defines a confidante as a person with whom one would discuss very personal and serious problems. Respondent's desire to change her relationship with men was assessed with a question from a study by Furstenberg (1983). It read, "on a scale from 0 to 5 where '1' is no change at all and '5' is a complete change, how much would you like to change your relationship with men?" Response options were not at all, a little, some, quite a lot, and complete change.

Male friend and relationship characteristics. Women who reported that they were involved at the time of the interview in an intimate, heterosexual relationship of at least three months duration, were asked when the relationship had begun; to describe their boy friend in terms of age, education, and employment status; and to identify methods used to resolve conflict. The Conflict Tactics Scale (CTS) (Straus, 1979) was used to gather information about how frequently each partner used each of 18 different behaviors when the couple had an argument during the three months preceding the interview. This frequently used inventory includes items that range from "discussing the issue calmly" to "using a knife or gun on the other person." The response options for each item are "never, once, twice, 3-5 times, 6-10 times, 11-20 times, and more than 20 times."

For purposes of this study, the items were used to construct four indices—Reason, Verbal/Symbolic Aggression, Physical Aggression, and Domestic Violence. Reason index items included: discussed the issue calmly, got information to back up (your/his) side of things, and brought in or tried to bring in someone to help settle things. Verbal/Symbolic index items included: insulted or swore at, sulked and/or refused to talk about it, stomped out of the room or house, cried, did or said something to be spiteful, threatened to hit or throw something, and threw or smashed or hit or kicked something (other than the partner). Physical Aggression index items included: threw something at the partner, pushed, grabbed, or shoved the partner, slapped the partner, hit or tried to hit the partner, and threatened the partner with a knife or gun. Domestic Violence index included: kicked, bit, or hit the partner with a fist, beat up the partner, and used a knife or gun on the partner. To construct the indices the response categories 3-5 times, 6-10 times, and 11-20 times were recoded to their midpoints and the category more than 20 was recoded to 25. Separate scores were then computed for the respondent and her boyfriend by adding the responses for each item in the index. Scores were divided into three categories: frequent use—used tactics 4 or more times during the three months preceding the interview; moderate use—used tactics 1 to 3 times during the three months preceding the interview; and no use—did not use any of the tactics during the three months preceding the interview.

FINDINGS

Dating Patterns—Their Prevalence

Participation in a nonmarital, heterosexual, intimate relationship of three months or longer duration seems to be the norm for this study's AFDC mothers. Ninety-five percent of the respondents reported having been involved in at least one such relationship, with 64% (176) of the women involved in one at the time of the interview.

For the women who were *not* involved in a relationship at the time of the interview (28%; n = 77), the norm was *not* to be dating or to be dating very infrequently. Of these women, sixty-eight percent said they were not dating at all and another 11% reported dating less than once per month. The "daters" (7%; n = 20) were going out once a month or more.

The Nonmarital, Intimate, Heterosexual Relationship — Its Characteristics

What are the characteristics of the intimate, nonmarital relationships? How long have they lasted? Who are their male friends?

Data on duration reveal that most relationships are not new: 64% had lasted for two years or more and another 13% had lasted for at least one year. The typical male friend was twenty-nine years old and 4.2 years older than the respondent. Sixty-five percent were employed. The vast majority, 96%, were reported not to be sharing the AFDC mother's residence; however, it is important to caution that respondents' may have been less than honest about living with their male friend because of the implications a 'yes' answer could have for continued AFDC eligibility.

Even though most respondents did not identify their male friends as their primary confidante, the relationships do not appear to be troubled. In fact, they may be quite satisfying. Data reveal:

a. A high degree of fidelity. Eighty-four percent of the involved women had had only one sexual partner during the year preceding the interview.
b. Fairly frequent intimacy. Fifty-two percent had had intercourse once/week or more during the year preceding the interview.
c. Little worry about relationship problems. Fifty percent of the women never worried about problems and 35% worried only occasionally or sometimes.
d. Optimism with regard to the relationship's future. Seventy-one percent expected the relationship to improve over the next two years.
e. Little desire to change the nature of their relationship with men. Only 14% of the women wanted to completely change their relationship or change it a lot.

Generally consistent with the above results are findings from the Conflict Tactics Scale indices (not displayed). They reveal that reasoning and verbal/symbolic aggression are more common as methods for handling conflict than physical aggression. Both partners of the majority of couples frequently (four or more times during the three months preceding the interview) used reason (58.7%) and/or verbal/symbolical aggression (59.1). On the other hand, both partners of only 9.7% of the couples frequently used physical aggression and not a single couple existed where both partners used abusive behavior even once.

Comparison of women and men with respect to each method for handling conflict suggests that women are probably more frequent users of all four methods than men, particularly the physically aggressive tactics. With respect to reasoning, 77.5% of the women versus 65.5% of the men used such tactics four or more times. With respect to verbal/symbolic aggression, 86.1% of the women and 61.5% of the men frequently used such tactics. With respect to physical aggression, 23.9% of the women and 13.1% of the men frequently used such tactics. And, finally, with respect to physical abuse, 3.6% of the women and 1.8% of the men frequently used such tactics.

Comparisons Among Groups

To determine if the women involved in long-term relationships differed from women who were not, comparisons were drawn with the women who were dating and those who were not dating with respect to demographic, fertility-related, and psychosocial characteristics. Because a large number of comparisons were made (22 in all), significance levels associated with individual tests within each of the three sets of characteristics were adjusted for multiple comparisons by dividing .05 by the number of tests. This adjustment holds the probability of a 'within set' Type I error to an alpha level of .05.

Even though the comparisons reveal mostly similarities (see Table 1), the differences that exist are informative. They show that the "daters" and the "not active daters" differ from women involved

Table 1

Comparison of Women Involved in Relationships at the Time of the Interview with Women Who Were Actively Dating and Women Who Were Not Actively Dating

Variables	Dating Status		
	Not Active (n=77)	Active Dating (n=20)	Intimate relationship (n=176)[1]
1. Demographic Variables			
Average age	27.4*	25.7	25.1
Average grade completed	11.0	11.3	11.1
Average time in years on AFDC	5.5	4.4	4.0
Percentage ever married	37.7*	25.0	20.5
Percentage black	80.5	75.0	90.9
Percentage ever employed	64.9	65.0	61.4
Percentage who attend religious			
services once/month or more	22.1	25.0	27.8
2. Psychosocial Variables			
Average self-esteem score	19.0	20.0	19.5
Average locus of control score	16.8	17.4	17.7
Average Beck Depression Score	11.0	8.6	8.9
Percentage with a confidante	87.0	90.0	88.6
Percentage of primary confidantes[a] that are			
lover	0.0	0.0	7.1
relative	73.1	55.6	73.1
friend	26.9	44.4	13.5
Percentage who believe it very			
likely that primary confidante			
would given them money[a]	89.2	100.0	90.4

Variables	Dating Status		
	Not Active (n=77)	Active Dating (n=20)	Intimate relationship (n=176)[1]

2. Psychosocial Variables

Percentage who want to change their
relationship with men

not at all or a little	52.0	50.0	64.2
some	22.1	25.0	21.0
a lot or completely	26.0	25.0	14.8

3. Fertility-Related Variables

Average age at first intercourse	16.2	15.4	15.7
Average age at first live birth	19.9	18.9	19.5
Average number of live births	2.2*	2.0	1.8
Percentage with 2 or more sexual partners during last year	30.5	70.6*	15.7
Percentage sexually active during 8 weeks prior to interview	47.6*	68.4*	96.4

1 Missing data may reduce some of the sample but never exceeds 5%.
a Among women who reported having at least one confidante. The primary
confidante is the first confidante identified by those women who reported
having more than one confidante.
b Among women who reported having intercourse during the eight weeks preceding
the interview.
c Among women who are not sterile.
* For demographic and psychosocial characteristics an asterisk (*) indicates a
significant test adjusting for multiple comparisons at a < .05 (equivalent to a
univariate tests at .05/7 = < .007. For fertility-related characteristics an
asterisk indicates a significant test adjusting for multiple comparisons at a <
.05 (equivalent to a univariate test at .05/8 = < .006. An asterisk beside a
value in column 1 (not actively dating) or column 2 (actively dating) indicates
that the comparison with women involved in intimate relationships at the time
of the interview is significant.

in intimate relationships in different ways. This divergent pattern of differences might be interpreted to suggest that inactive daters represent a different segment of the AFDC population than active daters and women involved in intimate relationships.

Least different from the women involved in intimate relationships are the 20 women who are actively dating. The two groups vary with respect to only two of the 22 characteristics. Active daters are more likely to have had two or more sexual partners during the year preceding the interview (70.6% versus 15.7%) and are less likely to have had sexual activity during the eight weeks preceding the interview (68% versus 96%). In all other ways the two groups of women are similar. In sum, the high degree of similarity between these two groups of women, the expected nature of the two differences that do exist, the past involvement of all 20 daters in at least one intimate relationship, and the fact that 10 of the 20 daters were dating only one man at the time of the interview suggest two conclusions. Daters may be in transition from one intimate relationship to another *and* daters and women involved in intimate relationships may be from the same subpopulation of AFDC recipients.

Relatively less similar to the women involved in intimate relationships are the women who are *not* actively dating. The two groups differ with respect to five of the 22 characteristics. The "inactive daters" are older, have had more live births, are more likely to have been married, are less likely to want more children, and, as might be expected, are less likely to have been sexually active during the eight weeks preceding the interview. The nature of the first four of these five differences suggests that nonactive daters may represent a different segment of the AFDC population — one with very different parenting experiences and future expectations — than the other two groups of women.

IMPLICATIONS FOR COUPLES WORK

The findings are some of the first that describe nonmarital, yet long-term relationships of AFDC mothers who are not known for child maltreatment. While many of the relationships are described as satisfactory, it is interesting to consider why no psycho-social benefit could be identified that derived from them. This may indicate that having such a relationship may help in ways that were not measured. It may also be that these black women (the majority in this sample) are a self-reliant group and/or that their needs are being met by family members rather than men in the community. Viable black families are often those that have maintained strong ties with their families (Hines, 1989). It may not be that these couples' relationships are not beneficial, but rather that uninvolved women are able to find life satisfaction in other ways.

These findings can inform practitioners about the normative expectations for these relationships and may help debunk popular myths. Specifically, many of the relationships are stable. There is a high level of fidelity as well as intimacy. Few women have worries about their relationship and most are optimistic that it will improve. What is most surprising was that when violence was present in the couples' relationship, it was more likely to have been perpetrated by the mother than by her male friend.

A number of interpretations can be given for this. First, are the expectations the mothers bring to the couple's relationship different than that of the male friend? Once an intimate long-term relationship has been established, she may be more likely to be frustrated by the behavior of the male friend than women who are only dating. Second, are men who become involved in long-term relationships less violent than other men, resulting in more female perpetrated violence? Third, violence between couples is often the result of tension (Rosenbaum and O'Leary, 1986). Are relationships among AFDC mothers more stressful for women than men. McGoldrick, Garcia-Preto, Hines, and Less (1989) point out that there are fewer black men than black women in the U.S. Does this inequity in numbers lead to increased frustration and tension in the relationship on the woman's part because of the possible feeling on the part of some men that they have more options for intimacy?

The mental health practitioner must explore these issues to see if they are affecting the nature of the relationship. In addition, the utilization of a confidante other than the male friend remains a viable consideration in treatment of the mother. These single mothers clearly benefit from the contact they have with relatives and others they feel they can trust and can be encouraged to maintain those relationships when appropriate.

As we have used the mother as the point of reference for this study, additional considerations can be offered that might be helpful to working with the male friend as part of the couple. Addressing the peripheral role that men are often forced to play when the mother is receiving AFDC speaks to, what we consider, the key relationship issue. These men are an unacknowledged part of the family. As such, they may often feel they are in a "one-down" position in relation to the mother as it is she that may have the steadier income. The father's role within the family must be made overt and clarified. Reframing his involvement to one in which he *is* playing an important role can help boost those situations where his self-esteem is low. Like most reframes, this involves an understanding of the couple's situation and a creative use of metaphor. Finally, finding other support systems for the male can assist him in reducing any sense of isolation he might be experiencing. This support may come in the form of work, neighborhood, church, or family relations.

The drawing of genograms to understand the variegated stressors on low-income families has been suggested as an appropriate first step in treatment (Hines, 1989; Boyd-Franklin, 1989). Meeting the concrete needs and working toward empowering the members of the couple to deal with systems impinging upon the couple can lay the ground work for future couples' work. For example, how fruitful can work on the couples' relationship be if the mother is being threatened with removal from her housing? If the mother is successful in her quest to assure housing for her family, that victory can give her the confidence to deal with relationship issues. With an understanding of the couple's context and with data on the viability of these relationships, mental health practitioners can fine-tune the work that they provide to a population that they have often underserved.

REFERENCES

Bahr, Stephen J. 1979. "The effects of welfare on marital stability and remarriage." *Journal of Marriage and the Family, 41*, 553-560.
Bane, M.J. and Ellwood, D.T. (1989). One fifth of the nation's children: Why are they poor? *Science, 245*, 1047-1953.

Beck, A. T. (1970). *Depression: Causes and Treatment*. Philadelphia, PA: University of Pennsylvania Press.

Boyd-Franklin, N. (1989). *Black families in therapy: A multi-systems approach*. N.Y.: Guilford.

Brown, G. W., & Harris, T. (1978). *Social Origins of Depression: A Study of Psychiatric Disorder in Women*. London, England: Tavistock.

Draper, Thomas W. (1981.) "On the relationship between welfare and marital stability: A research note." *Journal of Marriage and the Family, 43*, 293-299.

Furstenberg, F. (1983). Baltimore Study, Mother Questionnaire. Philadelphia, PA: Institute for Survey Research, Temple University.

Hines, P.M. (1989). The family life cycle of poor black families. Pages 513-544 in B. Carter and M. McGoldrick (eds.), *The changing family life cycle*. Boston: Allyn and Bacon.

Kotelchuck, M. (1982). Child abuse and neglect: prediction and misclassification. Pages 67-104 in Ray H. Starr, Jr. (ed.), *Child Abuse Prediction: Policy Implications*. Cambridge, MA: Ballenger.

McGoldrick, M. (1982). Normal families: An ethnic perspective. Pages 399-422 in F. Walsh (ed). *Normal family processes*. N.Y.: Guilford.

McGoldrick, M., Garcia-Preto, N., Hines, P.M., and Less, E. (1989). Ethnicity and women. Pages 169-199 in M. McGoldrick, C. Anderson, & F. Walsh (ed). *Women in families*. N.Y.: Norton.

Rank, Mark R. (1986). "Family structure and the process of exiting from welfare." *Journal of Marriage and the Family, 48*, 607-618.

Rank, Mark R. (1987). "The formation and dissolution of marriages in the welfare population." *Journal of Marriage and the Family, 49*, 15-20.

Robins, L. N., Helzer, J. E., Croughan, J., & Ratcliff, K. S. (1981). National Institute of Mental Health Diagnostic Interview Schedule: Its history, characteristics, and validity. *Archives of General Psychiatry, 38*, 381-389.

Robinson, B.E. (1988). Teenage pregnancy from the father's perspective. *American Journal of Orthopsychiatry, 58*, 46-51.

Rosenbaum, A. and O'Leary, K.D. (1986). The treatment of marital violence. Pages 385-405 in N.S. Jacobson and A.S. Gurman (eds.) *Clinical handbook of marital therapy*. N.Y.: Guilford.

Rosenberg, M. (1979). *Conceiving the Self*. New York: Basic Books.

Starr, R., Jr. (1982). A research-based approach to the prediction of child abuse. Pages 105-134 in Ray H. Starr, Jr. (ed.), *Child Abuse Prediction: Policy Implications*. Cambridge, MA: Ballenger Publishing Company.

Straus, M. (1979). Measuring intrafamily conflict and violence: The conflict tactics scales. *Journal of Marriage and the Family, 41*, 75-88.

Tanfer, K. (1983). National Study of Unmarried Young Women. Questionnaire and Interviewer's Instruction Manual. Philadelphia, PA: Institute for Survey Research, Temple University.

Tanfer, K. (1987.) "Patterns of premarital cohabitation among never-married women in the United States." *Journal of Marriage and the Family, 49*, 483-495.

Wallerstein, J. and Kelly, J. (1980). *Surviving the breakup*. New York: The Free Press.

Wolock, I. and Horowitz, B. (1977). Factors relating to levels of child care among families receiving public assistance in New Jersey. Final report to the National Center on Child Abuse and Neglect DHEW Grant 9-C-418.

Zuravin, S., and Greif, G. (1989). Normative and child-maltreating AFDC mothers. *Social Casework, 70,* 76-84.

Zuravin, S. and Taylor, R. (1987). Child care adequacy and family planning practices. Final report to the U.S. Department of Health and Human Services, Public Health Service, Office of Population Affairs for Grant FPR 000028-02-0.

Power Issues in Therapists:
An Interview with Virginia Satir

Sheldon Starr

[Early in 1985 I asked Virginia Satir if she was willing to be interviewed on videotape concerning her thinking about family therapy at that time and especially with regard to any ideas she might wish to share with the family therapy community. The interview took place on March 15, 1985 at Virginia's home in Menlo Park, CA. The transcript of the interview is 60 pages, and this is the *second* of a series of segments from that interview covering different themes.¹ This segment touches on the use and abuse of power in therapy.]

STARR: That brings up another issue I'm concerned about. I heard a well-known family therapist offhandedly say: "I think the field of family therapy is in the process of destroying itself." I'm not quite

Sheldon Starr, PhD was founder and director for 15 years of the Family Study Unit, a family therapy training and treatment program at the V.A. Medical Center, Palo Alto, CA when this interview was conducted. The first part of this interview appeared in "Coupling . . . What Makes Permanence?," The Haworth Press, Inc., 1991, also published as *Journal of Couples Therapy*, Volume 2, Number 3, 1991. Dr. Starr is presently Professor of Psychology (part time) at Pacific Graduate School of Psychology and is in private practice, both in Palo Alto, CA. His association with Virginia Satir spanned 25 years, first as student, then as associate and long-time friend. Correspondence may be sent to 801 Welch Road, #209, Palo Alto, CA 94304.

1. A highly condensed and edited summary of the entire interview appeared in the AFTA Newsletter, Fall 1985 and that version consisted of less than 20% of the interview.

[The use of brackets [ ] and italics are editorial additions for the purpose of clarity and emphasis.] S.S.

sure what he meant by that but I'm not so sure it did not refer to how we train people and how we do therapy from a technological point of view. What do you think?

SATIR: One of the worries I had at the beginning was I hoped that what we did in family therapy as we came to learn about it, was *not* to divide and figure out who was right, but rather to have an ongoing cooperative relationship in learning what [families] were because it's obvious that a family unit is not the same as an individual, even though there may be some parts that are the same. When we get into the family we [therapists] are bound to use our own messages and if we don't know what they are we're going to do bad things. What has disturbed me in the last six months is the many people, the consumers of the service who have told me what a terrible experience they had with a therapist, a family therapist — how they were put down, treated as objects, how they were asked to do crazy things and how things were just worse. That bothers me a lot. One of the things I think we need to do is to get together in an honest way, share what we've learned, and take a look at what it means.

STARR: Who? Who's the we?

SATIR: I'm talking about the people who teach therapy. I'm talking about people like Minuchin, Selvini, Norman Paul, Murry Bowen, myself, Jay Haley — people also that are up there (these aren't the only ones, Epstein, Gus Napier, Carl Whitaker) — to take a look at what we do and to see what part of it is semantics, what part of it have we seen together, what part have some of us seen [that others have not] and then to talk about what real change is about. How do I become a really effective agent?

STARR: Okay. I see some problems with that. My experience with family therapists is that as a group they are at least as competitive, self-serving, and non-collaborative as any other profession.

SATIR: It didn't used to be that way at the very beginning. It is now, you're right.

STARR: We know that staffs of Family Institutes have split up, that some [institutes] have gone down the drain because the people that were there quit talking to each other. Now, we might describe a family as dysfunctional if they were competitive and non-collaborative in some kind of effort together. Yet, that's the very thing that family therapists are themselves. Now shouldn't we know better?

SATIR: I'm going to tell you, absolutely we should know better! So the interesting question is: 'Why do we behave as though we don't know better?'

STARR: Do you have any ideas of what to do about it?

SATIR: Well I know what I'd do about it. . . .

STARR: You'd gather a group of family therapists together. . . .

SATIR: Well this is one of the things I'm talking about is how to do that. The part I didn't say is that you bring people together, [and] we act as agents to get those who are willing, to deal with this very issue you're talking about. See, I withdrew from this arena after awhile because I got tired of working with what I call "primadonna" relationships. I wanted to give something and I wanted to receive something, but one of the things, and no offense to anybody I hope, [was that] I was the *only woman* for so many years; there wasn't anybody else. And I went all around the world, did all my things and I *never* felt any real support from any of you guys. None of them! They had to deal with me but I didn't feel any real support from *any* of them![2] Anyway, that's kind of where it is. At this point in time I think you hit the nail right on the head. And let me tell you how that works. It's like, do what I say, not what I do.

STARR: Sure.

SATIR: And that's what the parent does. There are some family staffs, however, that I've been privileged to be invited to, and they are aware that they are having problems as a "family" and will call in somebody to work at it. But see, we do nothing with *philosophy of the self* in training. We don't look at the whole self-worth issue. I've been the only one that I know of that has put self-worth at the center of what's going on — the center for me, and the center for the people I'm working with. So, that again comes back to a way of viewing, and you know it also comes back to what you call your

---

2. Spoken emotionally in a hurt tone-of-voice.

own security. If two family therapists get together and they have to compete, that's not because they're family therapists, that's because they're competitive people. And what do you think is going to happen with them when they're working with families? They're going to do the same darned thing. And then what's going to happen is the families are going to get upset and do something and you know what's going to happen? Just what [happened] to individual therapy. You have these "impossible" patients [rather than "impossible" therapists].

STARR: Well, that's what I'm worried about too. Are we going to become disenchanted with Family Therapy just as therapists have become disenchanted with orthodox psychoanalysis? You know, that everything sounds good, but when it comes down to the bottom line we're not going to deliver the goods to the people who need it most.

SATIR: Well, see most of what I do, (you asked me at the beginning about me), is help people to connect with each other and to move beyond this kind of thing. Put in a nutshell, it is a *control problem. It's a power problem!* These kinds of control/power problems are based upon fear, fear I won't be valued or loved so I have to get out there and scratch.

STARR: Okay, so you're saying you see them [therapists] as living-out something from their own past in their role as professional

SATIR: Absolutely, and I don't think we're free of it.